The Plutarch Project, Volume One

The Plutarch Project, Volume One

Marcus Cato the Censor, Philopoemen, and Titus Flamininus

by

Anne E. White

The Plutarch Project, Volume One: Marcus Cato the Censor, Philopoemen, and Titus Flamininus
Copyright © 2015 by Anne E. White www.annewrites.ca

Cover design: Bryan White

Cover photograph: Addison Courthouse radio restored by Bryan White

All rights reserved. No part of this publication may be reproduced, stored in a retrieval system or transmitted in any form by any means, electronic, mechanical, photocopy, recording or otherwise, without the prior permission of the publisher, except as provided by Canadian copyright law.

ISBN-13 978-0-9947977-2-8

CONTENTS

Acknowledgements/Thanks vii

Introduction to the Plutarch Project ix

Why Plutarch? xi

Marcus Cato the Censor 1

    Lesson One 2

    Lesson Two 6

    Lesson Three 10

    Lesson Four 13

    Lesson Five 16

    Lesson Six 19

    Lesson Seven 21

    Lesson Eight 24

    Lesson Nine 28

    Lesson Ten 32

    Lesson Eleven 36

    Lesson Twelve 38

Philopoemen 43

    Lesson One 44

    Lesson Two 47

    Lesson Three 50

    Lesson Four 54

Lesson Five 57

Lesson Six 61

Lesson Seven 64

Lesson Eight 69

Lesson Nine 72

Lesson Ten 74

Lesson Eleven 79

Lesson Twelve 82

Titus Flamininus 87

Lesson One 88

Lesson Two 92

Lesson Three 97

Lesson Four 100

Lesson Five 104

Lesson Six 106

Lesson Seven 110

Lesson Eight 113

Lesson Nine 117

Lesson Ten 120

Lesson Eleven 124

Lesson Twelve 126

Bibliography 133

About the Author 134

Acknowledgements/Thanks

*Thank you to my daughters, my first reason to read Plutarch.
And to the AmblesideOnline families,
who brought the project to life.*

"But Theodorus Gaza, a man learned in the Latin tongue, and a great restorer of the Greek, who lived above two hundred years ago, deserves to have his suffrage set down in words at length; for the rest have only commended Plutarch more than any single author, but he has extolled him above all together.

"'Tis said that, having this extravagant question put to him by a friend, that if learning must suffer a general shipwreck, and he had only his choice left him of preserving one author, who should be the man he would preserve, he answered, Plutarch; and probably might give this reason, that in saving him, he should secure the best collection of them all." Arthur Hugh Clough, Preface to Plutarch's Lives (1859)

Introduction to the Plutarch Project

I am married to someone who specializes in taking the covers off things. Before Bryan, I didn't know so many things *had* insides.

Writing studies for *Plutarch's Lives* is a bit like watching my husband restore a 1934 Crosley Fiver radio. (It was one of the first radios you could just bring home from the store, plug in, and listen to.) He bought it refinished, but not in working order.

The schematic diagram didn't give values for the components. Anyone should be able to figure that out, right? The radio was put together (by hand) in the days before many electronic conventions were developed; before wires were colour-coded for positive, negative, etc. Tracing out the connections was like doing one of those picture puzzles with six fishing lines and one fish.

But that's what Bryan knows how to do, so he started taking the components apart (he took a photograph first just in case). He went into his stash of parts, replaced the resistors and capacitors, fixed the non-functioning power switch, and made it all work again.

Plutarch doesn't need me to make his *Lives* work. I am the first one to insist that I am not a classical scholar. To misquote Ben Jonson, I have one year of Latin and no Greek. About the only thing that qualified me to take this project on is that, like Bryan, I like to take covers off and see what's inside. What I have tried to do is make Plutarch more of a plug-in model than a workbench project.

In the thirteen years since the first study appeared on the AmblesideOnline[1] website, I have heard from many people who said, "I didn't know anything about Plutarch; I was afraid to do Plutarch; but now it's one of our favourite studies." One of the best stories I heard recently came from the leader of a co-op group in Tennessee that spent a number of weeks studying Plutarch's *Life of Alcibiades*, and then moved on to *Coriolanus*. At the end of the school year, the co-op students held a (reportedly heated) debate over the leadership qualties and the personal strengths and weaknesses of the two subjects. But that wasn't the end of it. A month later, during summer vacation, the mother of three of the students heard them still arguing the question of whether Alcibiades or Coriolanus would make a better President of the United States.

That's what you call engagement with the subject.

Translation Notes/Editing Caveat

These notes, and the accompanying text, are based on Thomas North's 1579 translation of Plutarch's *Lives of the Noble Greeks and Romans*, with some substitutions from John Dryden's 1683 translation [in brackets]. I have updated spelling, and occasionally punctuation. There are also a number of omissions, either for length or for suitability, which are *not* always noted. I have tried to be respectful to Plutarch's text, but have amplified and clarified where it seemed helpful for students and parents/teachers.

The format of the study notes is fairly simple. Each *Life* is divided into twelve lessons (as the AmblesideOnline terms are divided into twelve weeks). I have included vocabulary words and narration/study questions, but there is no requirement that you use them in a traditional classroom style. In fact, it's probably better if you don't. The vocabulary words are there only to save time on having to look things up, or to explain puzzles like why the Romans were paying debts with *asses* (an *as* was a coin). Those following Charlotte Mason's educational methods will want to include oral or written narration (telling back in the student's own words), and oral narration can take place more than once during a lesson. (I used to stop during a reading and ask whichever daughter was listening, "What just happened there?" With Plutarch's long sentences, even I wasn't always sure.) Sometimes I have suggested a "creative narration," such as an interview or a writing assignment.

Again, students don't need to answer every question; you don't even need to use the questions in the guide. They are just there as suggestions. It's better if the students ask the questions, at least some of the time.

Finally, you may notice that some of the questions come from a specifically Christian worldview. I do not apologize for that, but I do think it's fair to mention it. Those with other beliefs may find similar references within their own faith traditions.

Notes

1. AmblesideOnline is a free, online Charlotte Mason homeschooling curriculum, found at www.amblesideonline.org

Why Plutarch?

(reprinted from *Minds More Awake*)

The decision to include Plutarch's *Lives*—or not—or in what translation—becomes a kind of touchpoint for how we view (or do) a Charlotte Mason education. Shakespeare is easy; everyone knows Shakespeare, recognizes Shakespeare. Nobody argues with teaching Shakespeare. But Plutarch belongs much more unmistakably to Charlotte Mason. If homeschooling was the world and Charlotte Mason was Canada, Plutarch would be maple syrup. We need to ask, and it's a fair question, if this was just one of those quaint turn-of-the-century ideas, like making Smyrna rugs for handicrafts; if Plutarch's *Lives* is essential in itself, or if what it offers could much more easily be acquired through newer books. Why did Charlotte Mason include this particular piece of antiquity?

Here are some of the reasons that Mason gave herself, or that were noted by her colleagues:

1) In the preface to *Ourselves*, she wrote that the novels of Sir Walter Scott and Plutarch's *Lives* were "sources that fall within everybody's reading." This is obviously not the case now, but at one time, Plutarch was considered common currency. Shakespeare read Plutarch. Abraham Lincoln read Plutarch. Frankenstein's monster read Plutarch. Ralph Waldo Emerson begins his essay on Plutarch with the words, "It is remarkable that of an author so familiar as Plutarch, not only to scholars, but to all reading men..." Plutarch is not studied in most contemporary schools, at least below university level, but he was less obscure in previous eras than we may realize.

2) Similarly, the introduction of Plutarch at what seems a younger-than-necessary age was explained in *Parents and Children*[1] as part of a plan that brings a child to the world's library door, and offers him the key to its contents. (It is worth noting that Mason mentions only two books in that passage: *Tanglewood Tales* for young children, and then Plutarch's *Lives*.) We don't just hand the child these books; we read them to him, but without too much

explanation, a gift from one book-loving friend to another. We read, he narrates, we discuss, but we do not limit what he learns to our own ideas about it. My own prepared notes might seem to be at cross-purposes with Mason's "pick it up and read" attitude, but I justify them with the hope that they will encourage those of us (including myself) who did not grow up with Plutarch...

3) As well as an early beginning to literature and the habit of reading in general, Plutarch offers "the best preparation for the study of Grecian or of Roman history."[2] Note that Mason said preparation for history, not history itself. It is a familiarizing, a paving of the way. After reading several *Lives*, we begin to recognize not only the characters, but also common events such as the annual election of Roman consuls...

4) The book *In Memoriam* says that Charlotte Mason lived during an age that was fascinated by history, but that her "standards of judgement were ethical" and that "greatness in goodness was her ideal..."[3] Miss Ambler, the author of a *Parents' Review* article on teaching Plutarch, agreed:

> We need, however, to have more than a goal in view; we need to know the way to reach it. We know what is necessary for a good citizen, and we wish to send the children out equipped for service with high ideals and the courage to live up to them.[4]

Notes

1. Charlotte Mason, *Parents and Children*, pp.231-232.

2. Charlotte Mason, *Home Education*, p.286.

3. *In Memoriam*, Parents' National Educational Union, 1923. http://www.amblesideonline.org/CM/InMemoriam.html

4. Miss M. Ambler, "'Plutarch's Lives' as Affording Some Education as a Citizen," *The Parents' Review*, 12 (1901): 521-527, AmblesideOnline

Marcus Cato the Censor

"In order to do all this we give the life stories of great men, the first great writer of which, Plutarch, has left us a wonderful store-house of great ideas and examples, showing how the life of the individual is the life of the state, and that where private standards are high or low, public morality is upheld or falls; thus it would be possible to trace much of the gradual break-down of the Roman military colonies to the example of "Mark Antony," and two such lives as those of Cato the Censor and Alcibiades will do much to teach future generations what good or evil one man can do for his times." (*The Parents' Review*) [1]

Who was Marcus Cato?

Marcus Porcius Cato (234 BC-149 BC) was a Roman statesman, also called Cato Censorius (the Censor), Cato Sapiens (the Wise), Cato Priscus (the Ancient), Cato Major, or Cato the Elder.

He is the great-grandfather of Cato the Younger, who is mentioned both in the story of Julius Caesar, and at the end of this Life.

What is a Censor?

The office of censor was one of the highest-ranking positions in Rome, allowed only to those who had previously been consul. Two censors were usually elected, because there were two consuls. Their duties are explained in Lesson Eight.

Lesson One

Introduction

Marcus Cato was a Roman "upstart." He came from an ancient but not a noble family, and throughout his life he prided himself on the fact that he had "risen by virtue."

Vocabulary

> **fell:** evil, destructive
>
> **utterance:** the ability to speak well
>
> **sway:** power
>
> **victuals:** food
>
> **overtriumphed thrice:** been honoured three times for battle victories
>
> **hard by Cato:** near Cato's house

Reading

Marcus Cato and his ancestors were (as they say) of the city of Thusculum: but before he went unto the wars, and dealt in matters of the commonwealth, he dwelt and lived in the country of the Sabines, upon certain land his father left him. And though many of his ancestors were known to have been obscure: yet he himself did highly commend his father Marcus, by bearing his name, and saying he was a soldier, and had served valiantly in the field. And he telleth also of another Cato that was his great grandfather, who for his valiant service had been oft rewarded of the generals, with such honourable gifts, as the Romans did use to give unto them, that had done some famous act in any battle: and how that he having lost five horses of service in the wars, the value of the same were restored to him again in money of the common treasure, because he had shewed himself trusty and valiant for the commonwealth. And where they had a common speech at Rome to call them *upstart*, that were no gentlemen born, but did rise by virtue: it fortuned Cato to be called one of them. And for his part, he did confess it, that he was of the first of the house that ever had honour, and office of state: but by reason of the noble acts and good service of his ancestors, he maintained he was very ancient. He was called at the beginning after his third name, Priscus: but afterwards by reason of his great wisdom and experience, he was surnamed Cato, because the Romans call a wise man, and him that hath seen much, Cato. He was somewhat given to be red-faced, and had a pair of staring eyes in his head, as this man telleth us, that for ill will wrote these verses of him after his death:

> Pluto (the god) which rules the furies infernally
> will not receive the damned ghost, of Porcius in his hall:
> his saucy coppered nose, and fiery staring eyes,
> his common slanderous tales, which he did in this world devise,
> made Pluto stand in dread that he would brawl in hell,
> although his bones were dry and dead, on earth he was so **fell**.

[Note: Dryden translates "staring eyes" as "gray eyes," so take whichever you prefer.]

Furthermore, touching the disposition of his body, he was marvellous strong and lusty, and all because he did use to labour and toil even from his youth, and to live sparingly, as one that was ever brought up in the wars from his youth: so that he was of a very good constitution, both for strength of body, as for health also. As for **utterance**, he esteemed it as a second body, and most necessary gift, not only to make men honest, but also as a thing very requisite for a man that should bear **sway** and authority in the commonwealth. He practised to speak well in little villages near home, whither he went many times to plead men's causes in courts judicial, that would retain him of counsel: so as in short time he became a perfect pleader, and had tongue at will, and in process of time became an excellent orator.

After he was thus well known, they that were familiar with him began to perceive a grave manner and behaviour in his life, and a certain noble mind in him, worthy to be employed in matters of state and great importance, and to be called into the commonwealth. For he did not only refuse to take fees for his pleading, and following the causes he maintained: but furthermore made no reckoning of the estimation he won by that manner and practise, as though that was not the only mark he shot at.

But his desire reached further, rather to win himself fame by service in the wars, and by valiant fighting with his enemy: than with such a quiet and pleasing manner of life. Insomuch as when he was but a young stripling in manner, he had many cuts upon his breast, which he had received in diverse battles and encounters against the enemies. For he himself writeth, that he was but seventeen years old, when he went first unto the wars, which was about the time of Hannibal's chief prosperity, when he [*Hannibal and the Carthaginian army*] spoiled and destroyed all Italy. So when he came to fight, he would strike lustily, and never stir foot nor give back, and would look cruelly upon his enemy, and threaten him with a fearful and terrible voice, which he used himself, and wisely taught other also to use the like. For such countenances, said he, many times do fear the enemies more, than the sword ye offer them. When he went any journey, he ever marched afoot, and carried his armour upon his back, and had a man waiting on him that carried his **victuals** with him, with whom he was never angry (as they say) for anything he had prepared for his dinner or supper, but did help to dress it himself for the most part, if he had any leisure, when he had done the duty of a private soldier in fortifying the camp, or such other needful business. All the while he was abroad in service in the wars, he never drank other than clean water, unless it were when he found he was not well, and then he would take a little vinegar: but if he saw he were weak, he would then drink a little wine.

Now it fortuned, that Manius Curius the Roman, who had **overtriumphed thrice**, had a pretty house and land **hard by Cato**, where he kept in times past, which Cato for a walk would visit oft. And he [Cato] considering how little land he [Curius] had to his house, and what a little house he had withal, and how poorly it was built, wondered with himself what manner of man Curius had been, that having been the greatest man of Rome in his time, and having subdued the mightiest nations and people of all Italy, and driven King Pyrrhus also out of the same: yet himself with his own hands did manure that little patch of ground, and dwell in so poor and small a farm. Whether notwithstanding, after his three triumphs, the Samnites sent their ambassadors to visit him, who found him by the fireside [boiling turnips], and presented him a marvellous deal of gold from their state and communality. But Curius returned them again with their gold, and told them, that such as were contented with that supper, had no need of gold nor silver: and that for his part, he thought it greater honour to command them that had gold, than to have it himself. Cato remembering these things to himself, went home again, and began to think upon his house, of his living, of his family and servants, and also of his expenses: and to cut all superfluous charges, and fell himself to labour with his own hands, more than ever he had done before.

Furthermore, when Fabius Maximus took the city of Tarentum again, Cato served under him being very young, where he fell into familiar acquaintance with Nearchus the Pythagorian philosopher, in whom he took marvellous delight to hear him talk of Philosophy. Which Nearchus held the same opinion of pleasure, that Plato did, by calling it the sweet poison and chiefest bait to allure men to ill: and saying that the body was the first plague unto the soul, and that her only health, remedy, and purgation stood upon rules of reason, good examples and contemplations, that drive sinful thoughts and carnal pleasures of the body, far off from her. Cato moreover gave himself much to sobriety and temperance, and framed himself to be contented with little.

They say he fell in his very old age to the study of the Greek tongue, and to read Greek books, and that he profited somewhat by Thucydides, but much more by Demosthenes, to frame his matter, and also to be eloquent. Which plainly appeareth, in all his books and writings, full of authorities, examples, and stories taken out of Greek authors: and many of his sentences and morals, his adages and quick answers, are translated out of the same word for word.

Narration and Discussion

Where did Cato get some of his early ideas about life?

Is it Scriptural to think that our bodies are "plagues unto our souls" and that therefore pleasure is evil? Where do we draw the line between positive and negative, just enough and too much?

Discuss this sentence: "But Curius returned them again with their gold, and told them, that such as were contented with that supper, had no need of gold nor silver: and that for his part, he thought it greater honour to command them that had gold, than to have it himself." The Greeks had a similar story: "A friend of Diogenes visited him and found him eating a dinner of lentils. The friend was a courtier in the court of the king. He said to Diogenes, 'If you would learn to flatter, you would not have to eat lentils.' Diogenes replied, 'And if you would learn to eat lentils you would not have to flatter.'"

Lesson Two

Introduction

In this lesson we meet Lucius Valerius Flaccus, a mentor and lifelong friend to Cato. We also hear about Quintus Fabius Maximus (Plutarch's *Life of Fabius*), and about Scipio.

Vocabulary

towardly: promising

board: dinner table

griffe: young plant, sprout

to practise: to practise law

passed not for the malice and evil will of Scipio the Great: Dryden translates this "he did not hesitate to oppose Scipio."

diverse: many people

was waxen now: had increased in greatness

straitness: narrowness

seigniory: authority, domain

pulers: whiners

cater: obscure word meaning, in this case, a purchaser of goods

as (plural, asses): a Roman coin

apter: more likely

Reading

Now there was a noble man of Rome at that time, one of great authority, and a deep wise man besides, who could easily discern buds of virtue sprouting out of any **towardly** youth, who was of a good and honourable disposition to help forward, and to advance such. His name was Valerius Flaccus, a near neighbour unto Cato, who was informed by his servants of Cato's strange life, how he would be doing in his ground with his own hands: and how he would be gone every day betimes in the morning to little villages thereabout, to plead men's causes that prayed his counsel, and that when he had done, he would come home again: and if it were in winter, that he would but cast a little coat on his shoulders, and being summer he would go out bare, naked to the waist, to work in his ground among his servants and other workmen: and would besides, sit and eat with them together at one **board**, and drink as they did. Moreover, they told him also a world of such manners and fashions which he used, that shewed [him] to be a marvellous plain man, without pride and of a good nature. Then they told him what notable wise sayings and grave sentences they heard him speak. Valerius Flaccus hearing this report of him, willed his men one day to pray him to come to supper to him. Who falling in acquaintance with Cato, and perceiving he was of a very good nature, and well given, and that he was a good **griffe** to be set in a better ground: he persuaded him to come to Rome, and **to practise** there in the assembly of the people, in the common causes and affairs of the commonweal. Cato followed his counsel, who having been no long practiser among them, did grow straight into great estimation, and won him many friends, by reason of the causes he took in hand to defend: and was the better preferred and taken also, by means of the special favour and countenance Valerius Flaccus gave him.

For first of all, by voice of the people he was chosen tribune of the soldiers (to say, chosen colonel of a thousand footmen), and afterwards was made treasurer [*quaestor*]: and so went forwards, and grew to so great credit and authority, as he became Valerius Flaccus' companion in the chiefest offices of state, being chosen consul with him, and then censor.

But to begin withal, Cato made choice of Quintus Fabius Maximus; above all the Senators of Rome, Cato followed and gave himself to follow him altogether: and not so much for the credit and estimation Fabius Maximus was of, (who therein exceeded all the Romans of that time) as for the modesty and discreet government he saw in him, whom he determined to follow, as a worthy mirror and example.

At which time Cato **passed not for the malice and evil will of Scipio the Great,** who did strive at that present being but a young man, with the authority and greatness of Fabius Maximus, as one that seemed to envy his rising and greatness. For Cato being sent treasurer with Scipio, when he undertook the journey into Africa, and perceiving Scipio's bountiful nature and disposition to large gifts without mean to the soldiers: he told him plainly he did not so much hurt the commonwealth in wasting their treasure, as he did great harm in changing the ancient manner of their ancestors: who used to be contented with little, but he taught them to spend their superfluous money (all necessaries provided for) in vain toys and trifles, to serve their pleasure. Scipio made him answer, he would have no treasurer should control him in that sort, nor that should look so narrowly to his expenses: for his intent was to go to the wars, with full sails as it were, and that he would (and did also determine to) make the state privy to all his doings, but not to the money he spent. Cato hearing this answer, returned with speed out of Sicily unto Rome, crying out with Fabius Maximus in open Senate, that Scipio spent infinitely, and that he tended of riot, plays, comedies, and wrestlings, as if he had not been sent to make wars, invasions, and attempts upon their enemies. Upon this complaint the Senate appointed certain tribunes of the people, to go and see if their informations were true: and finding them so, that they should bring him back again to Rome. But Scipio shewed far otherwise to the commissioners that came thither, and made them see apparent victory, through the necessary preparation and provision he had made for the wars: and he confessed also, that when he had dispatched his great business, and was at any leisure, he would be privately merry with his friends: and though he was liberal to his soldiers, yet that made him not negligent of his duty and charge in any matter of importance. So Scipio took shipping, and sailed towards Africa, whither he was sent to make war.

Now to return to Cato. He daily increased still in authority and consequence, his credit by means of his eloquence, so that **diverse** called him the Demosthenes of Rome: howbeit the manner of his life pains more estimation, than his eloquence. For all the youth of Rome did seek to attain to his eloquence and commendation of words, and one envied another which of them should come nearest: but few of them would [defile] their hands with any labour as their forefathers did, and make a light supper and dinner, without fire or provision, or would be content with a mean gown, and a poor lodging, and finally would think it more honourable to defy fancies and pleasures, than to have and enjoy them, because the state **was waxen now** of such power and wealth, as it could no more retain the ancient discipline, and former austerity and **straitness** of life it used: but by reason of the largeness of their dominion and **seigniory**, and the numbers of people and nations that were become their subjects, it was even forced to receive a medley of sundry country fashions, examples, and manners. This was a cause, why in reason men did so greatly wonder at Cato's virtue, when they saw other[s] straight wearied with pains and labour, tenderly brought up like **pulers**: and Cato on the other side never overcome, either with the one or with the other, no not in his youth, when he most coveted honour, nor in his age also when he was gray-headed and bald, after his consulship and triumph, but like a conqueror that had gotten the mastery, he would never give over labour even unto his dying day. For he writeth himself, that there never came gown on his back that cost him above a hundred pence, and that his hinds and workmen always drank no worse wine, when he was consul and general of the army, than he did himself: and that his **cater** never bestowed in meat for his supper, above thirty **asses** [*see note above*] of Roman money, and yet he said it was, because he might be the stronger, and **apter** to do service in the wars for his country and the commonwealth.

9

Narration and Discussion

What most impressed Valerius Flaccus about Cato?

Did Cato choose a good role model in the Senate?

Explain the argument that Cato had with Scipio, about "unnecessary" military expenses. Which side would you take? How did Scipio eventually win his case?

Lesson Three

Introduction

This lesson shows examples of Cato's extreme thrift, including something with which Plutarch disagrees: his attitude towards "worn-out" slaves.

Vocabulary

> **neatherd:** cowherd
>
> **arable:** farmable
>
> **ortyard:** orchard
>
> **cast:** no longer useful
>
> **spoiled in our service**: worn out with work

Reading

He said furthermore, that being heir to one of his friends that died, he had a piece of tapestry by him with a deep border, which they called then the Babylonian border, and he caused it straight to be sold: and that of all his houses he had abroad in the country, he had not one wall plastered, nor rough cast.
 Moreover he would say, he never bought bondman or slave dearer

than a thousand five hundred pence, as one that sought not for fine made men, and goodly personages, but strong fellows that could away with pains, as carters, horsekeepers, **neatherds**, and such like: and again he would sell them when they were old, because he would not keep them when they could do no service. To conclude, he was of opinion, that a man bought any thing dear, that was for little purpose: yea, though he gave but a farthing for it, he thought it too much to bestow so little, for that which [was] needed not. He would have men purchase houses, that had more store of **arable** land and pasture, than of fine **ortyards** or gardens. Some say, he did thus, for very misery and covetousness: other think, and took it that he lived so sparingly, to move others by his example to cut of all superfluity and waste. Nevertheless, to sell slaves in that sort, or to turn them out of doors when you have had the service of all their youth, and that they are grown old, as you use brute beasts that have served whilst they may for age: methinks that must needs proceed of too severe and greedy nature, that hath no longer regard or consideration of humanity, than whilst one is able to do another good.

For we see, gentleness goeth further than justice. For nature teacheth us to use justice only unto men, but gentleness sometimes is shewed unto brute beasts: and that cometh from the very fountain and spring of all courtesy and humanity, which should never dry up in any man living. For to say truly, to keep **cast** horses **spoiled in our service**, and dogs also not only when they are whelps, but when they be old: be even tokens of love and kindness. As the Athenians made a law, when they builded their temple called Hecatompedon: that they should suffer the [mules] that did service in their carriages about the building of the same, to graze everywhere, without let or trouble of any man. And they say, there was one of those moils [*mules*] thus turned at liberty, that came of herself to the place to labour, going before all the other draught beasts, that drew up carts laden towards the castle, and kept them company, as though she seemed to encourage the rest to draw: which the people liked so well in the poor beast, that they appointed she should be kept whilst she lived, at the charge of the town.

And yet at this present are the graves of Cimon's mares to be seen, that won him thrice together the game of the horse race at the games Olympian, and they are hard by the grave of Cimon himself.

We hear of diverse also that had buried their dogs they brought up in their house, or that waited on them: as among other old Xanthippus buried his dog on the top of a cliff, which is called the Dog's Pit till this day. For when the people of Athens did forsake their city at the coming down of Xerxes, this dog followed his master, swimming in the sea by his galley's side, from the firm land, unto the Isle of Salamina [*Salamis*].

And there is no reason, to use living and sensible things, as we would use an old shoe or a rag: to cast it out upon the dunghill when we have worn it, and can serve us no longer. For if it were for no respect else, but to use us always to humanity: we must ever show ourselves kind and gentle, even in such small points of pity. And as for me, I could never find in my heart to sell my draught ox that had plowed my land a long time, because he could plow no longer for age: and much less my slave to sell him for a little money, out of the country where he had dwelt a long time, to pluck him from his old trade of life wherewith he was best acquainted, and then specially, when he shall be as unprofitable for the buyer, as also for the seller.

But Cato on the other side gloried, that he left his horse in Spain he had served on in the wars during his consulship, because he would not put the commonwealth to the charge of bringing of him home by sea into Italy. Now a question might be made of this, and probable reason of either side, whether this was nobleness, or a niggardliness in him: but otherwise to say truly, he was a man of a wonderful abstinence. For when he was general of the army, he never took allowance but after three bushels [of] wheat a month of the commonwealth, for himself and his whole family: and but a bushel and half of barley a day, to keep his horse and other beasts for his carriage.

On a time when he was praetor, the government of Sardinia fell to his lot. And where the other praetors before him had put the country to exceeding great charge, to furnish them with tents, bedding, clothes, and such like stuff, and burdened them also with a marvellous train of servants and their friends that waited on them, putting them to great expense-of feasting and banqueting of them: Cato in contrary manner brought down all that excess and superfluity, unto a marvellous near and incredible saving. For when he went to visit the cities, he came afoot to them, and did not put them to a penny charge for himself: and had only one officer, or bailiff of the state, that waited on him, and carried his gown and a cup with him, to offer up wine to the goddess in his sacrifices.

But though he came thus simply to the [Sardinian] subjects, and eased them of their former charges, yet he shewed himself severe and bitter to them in matters concerning justice: and spared no man, in any commandment or service for the state and commonwealth. For he was therein so precise, that he would not bear with any little fault. So by this means, he brought the Sardinians under his government, both to love and fear the Empire of Rome, more than ever they did before.

Narration and Discussion

What are Plutarch's arguments against Cato's particular brand of "thrift?" Are there any applications of this for us today?

Lesson Four

Introduction

This lesson gives us "certain of Cato's notable sayings and sentences."

Vocabulary

meet: proper

could make men water their plants: could move them to tears

orators: those who make public speeches

corn: grain

wether: sheep

with some better discretion: Dryden translates this "sparingly"

all at a clap: all at once

to Epaminondas, to Pericles, etc: these were not kings but statesmen, but they are being praised as more trustworthy than kings

Reading

For his grace both in speaking and writing did rightly shew himself: because it was pleasant, and yet grave: sweet and fearful: merry and severe: sententious, and yet familiar: such as is **meet** to be spoken. And he was to be compared, as Plato said, unto Socrates: who at the first sight seemed a plain simple man to them that knew him not outwardly, or else a pleasant taunter or mocker: but when they did look into him, and found him thoroughly, they saw he was full of grave sentences, goodly examples, and wise persuasions, that he **could make men water their plants** that heard him, and lead them as he would by the ear. Therefore I can not see any reason that moves men to say, Cato had Lysias's grace and utterance. Notwithstanding, let us refer it to their judgements that make profession to discern **orators'** graces and styles: for my part I shall content myself to write at this present, only certain of his notable sayings and sentences, persuading myself that men's manners are better discerned by their words, than by their looks, and so do many think.

On a time he seeking to dissuade the people of Rome, which would needs make a thankful distribution of **corn** unto every citizen, to no purpose: began to make an oration with this preface: It is a hard thing (my Lords of Rome) to bring the belly by persuasion to reason, that hath no ears.

And another time, reproving the ill government of the city of Rome, he said: it was a hard thing to keep up that state, where a little fish was sold dearer than an ox.

He said also that the Romans were like a flock of sheep. For sayeth he, as every **wether** when he is alone, doth not obey the shepherd, but when they are all together they one follow another for love of the foremost: even so are you, for when you are together, you are all contented to be led by the noses by such, whose counsel not a man alone of you would use in any private cause of your own.

And talking another time of the authority the women of Rome had over their husbands. He said: Other men command their wives, and we command men, and our wives command us.

But this last of all, he borrowed of Themistocles' pleasant sayings. For his son making him do many things by means of his mother, he told his wife one day: saying, The Athenians command all Greece, I command the Athenians, you command me, and your son ruleth you. I pray you therefore bid him use the liberty he hath **with some better discretion**, fool...as he is, since he can do more by that power and authority, than all the Grecians besides.

He said also that the people of Rome did not only delight in diverse sorts of purple, but likewise in diverse sorts of exercises. For said he, as diverse commonly dye that color they see best esteemed, and is most pleasant to the eye: even so the lusty youths of Rome do frame themselves to such exercise, as they see yourselves most like, and best esteem. He continually advised the Romans, that if their power and greatness came by their virtue and temperance, they should take heed they became no changelings, nor wax worse: and if they came to that greatness by vice and violence, that then they should change to better, for by that means he knew very well they had attained to great honour and dignity.

[To a man] that had unthriftily sold his lands which his father had left him, lying upon the sea side: he pointed unto them with his finger, and made as though he wondered how he came to be so great a man, that he was stronger than the sea. For that which the sea hardly consumeth, and eateth into, by little and little a long time: he had consumed it **all at a clap**.

Another time when King Eumenes was come to Rome, the Senate entertained him marvellous honourably, and the noblest citizens did strive, envying one another, who should welcome him best. But Cato in contrary manner shewed plainly, that he did suspect all this feasting and entertainment, and would not come at it. When one of his familiar friends told him, I marvel why you fly from King Eumenes' company, that is so good a Prince, and loves the Romans so well. Yea, said he, let it be so, but for all that, a king is no better than a ravening beast that lives of the prey: neither was there ever any king so happy, that deserved to be compared **to Epaminondas, to Pericles, to Themistocles, nor to Manius Curius, or to Hamylcar, surnamed Barca.**

They say his enemies did malice him, because he used commonly to rise before day, and did forget his own business to follow matters of state. And he affirmed, that he had rather lose the reward of his well doing, than not to be punished for doing of evil: and that he would bear with all other [people who were] offending ignorantly, but not with himself.

He said also, that wise men did learn and profit more by fools, than fools did by wise men. For wise men said he, do see the faults fools commit, and can wisely avoid them: but fools never study to follow the example of wise men's doings.

These be his wise sayings we find written of him, whereby we may the easilier conjecture his manners and nature.

Narration and Discussion

How was Cato's plain, simple manner of public speaking deceiving?

"On a time he seeking to dissuade the people of Rome, which would needs make a thankful distribution of corn unto every citizen, to no purpose: began to make an oration with this preface: It is a hard thing (my Lords of Rome) to bring the belly by persuasion to reason, that hath no ears." It sounds at first as if Cato is in sympathy with the poor people, saying that you can't feed bellies with speeches. But since Plutarch says that Cato was in fact not in favour of this handout, what did he mean by that?

Why did Cato say that wise men learn and profit more by fools, than the other way around? How does that relate to what was said (at the beginning of the lesson) about Socrates?

Lesson Five

Introduction

This part of the story takes place during Cato's consulship. Cato became the governor of Spain, which means that he had to go there and put down a rebellion. In spite of his tightwad tendencies, he decided it was worthwhile to hire some assistance for this job.

Vocabulary

environed: surrounded

marches: borders

razed: pulled down

He was no sooner entered into his charge: He was no sooner appointed to this position

Reading

Now, and when he was chosen consul with his friend Valerius Flaccus, the government of Spain fell to his lot. Here, having subdued many people by force of arms, and won others also by friendly means: suddenly there came a marvellous great army of the barbarous people against him, and had **environed** him so, as he was in marvellous danger, either shamefully to be taken prisoner, or to be slain in the field. Wherefore, he sent presently unto the Celtiberians, to pray aid of them, who were next neighbours unto the **marches** where he was. These Celtiberians did ask him two hundred talents to come and help him: but the Romans that were about him, could not abide to hire the barbarous people to defend them. Then Cato told them straight, there was no hurt in it, nor any dishonour unto them. For said he, if the field be ours, then we shall pay their wages we promised, with the spoil and money of our enemies: and if we lose it, then ourselves and they lie by it, being left neither man to pay, nor yet any to ask it.

In the end he won the battle, after a sore conflict, and after that time he had marvellous good fortune. For Polybius writeth, that all the walls of the cities that were on this side the river of Baetis, were by his commandment **razed** all in one day, which were many, and full of good soldiers. Himself writeth, that he took more cities in Spain, than he remained there days: and it is no vain boast, if it be true that is written, that there were four hundred cities of them.

Now, though the soldiers under him had gotten well in this journey, and were rich, yet he caused a pound weight of silver to be given to every soldier besides: saying, he liked it better that many should return home with silver in their purses, than a few of them with gold only. But for himself, he affirmed: that of all the spoil gotten of the enemies, he never had, from anything, saving that which he took in meat and drink. And yet, sayeth he, I speak it not to reprove them that grow rich by such spoils: but because I would contend in virtue rather with the best, than in money with the richest, or in covetousness with the most virtuous.

Now while Cato was in Spain, Scipio that was his enemy, and sought to hinder the course of his prosperity, and [who was] to have the honour of conquering all the rest of Spain: he made all the friends he could to the people, [so that he would] be chosen [governor] in Cato's place. **He was no sooner entered into his charge**, but he made all the possible speed he could to be gone, that he might make Cato's authority cease the sooner. Cato hearing of his hasty coming, took only five ensigns of footmen, and five hundred horsemen to attend upon him home: with the which, in his journey homeward, he overcame a people in Spain called the Lacetanians, and took six hundred traitors also that were fled from the Romans' camp to their enemies, and did put to death every mother's child of them. Scipio storming at that, said Cato did him wrong. But Cato to mock him finely, said: it was the right way to bring Rome to flourish, when nobleborn citizens would not suffer meanborn men, and upstarts as himself was, to go before them in honour: and on the other side when meanborn men would contend in virtue, with those that were of noblest race, and far above them in calling. For all that, when Cato came to Rome, the Senate commanded that nothing should be changed nor altered otherwise, than Cato had appointed it, whilst he was in his office.

So that the government for which Scipio made such earnest suit in Spain, was a greater disgrace unto him, than it was unto Cato: because he passed all his time and office in peace, having no occasion offered him to do any notable service worthy of memory.

Narration and Discussion

What accidental adventure did Cato have on his way home from the battle in Spain? How did this cause more conflict with Scipio?

"So that the government for which Scipio made such earnest suit in Spain, was a greater disgrace unto him, than it was unto Cato: because he passed all his time and office in peace..." Why was it a disgrace (in Roman terms) for the governor of a province to spend his time in peace?

Lesson Six

Introduction

This is the first of two lessons describing a very exciting adventure, with Cato leading a multi-national campaign against King Antiochus at Thermopylae.

Vocabulary

> **the honour to triumph:** been publicly honoured for his military success
>
> **marches:** borders
>
> **the compass [and circuit] the Persians had fetched about etc.:** at the first Battle of Thermopylae, long before this, the Persians used a roundabout (secret) route to get into Greece
>
> **lewd:** worthless, vile (older meanings)
>
> **to tarry him there**: to wait for him there

Reading

Furthermore, Cato after he had been consul, and had granted to him **the honour to triumph**: did not as many others do, that seek not after virtue, but only for worldly honour and dignity. Who, when they have been called to the highest offices of state, as to be consuls, and have also granted them the honour to triumph: do then leave to deal any more in matters of state, and dispose themselves to live [quietly] at home, and not to trouble themselves anymore. Now Cato, far otherwise behaved himself. For he would never leave to exercise virtue, but began afresh, as if he had been but a young novice in the world, and as one greedy of honour and reputation, and to take as much pains and more than he did before.

For, to pleasure his friends or any other citizen, he would come to the marketplace, and plead their causes for them that required his counsel, and go with his friends also into the wars. As he went with Tiberius Sempronius the consul, and was one of his lieutenants at the conquest of the country of Thrace, and unto the provinces adjoining to the river of Danube upon those **marches**.

After that, he was in Greece also, colonel of a thousand footmen, under Manius Aquilius, against King Antiochus surnamed the Great, who made the Romans as much afraid of him, as ever they were of Hannibal. For, when he [Antiochus] had conquered all the regions and provinces of Asia...and had subdued many barbarous and warlike nations: he was so proud hearted, as he would needs have wars with the Romans, whom he knew to be the only worthy men, and best able to fight with him. So he made some honest show and pretence of wars, saying: it was to set the Grecians at liberty, who had no cause thereof, considering they lived after their own laws, and were but lately delivered from the bondage of King Philip, and of the Macedonians, through the goodness of the Romans.

Notwithstanding, he came out of Asia into Greece with a marvellous great army, and all Greece was straight in arms and in wonderful danger, because of the great promises and large hopes the governors of diverse cities (whom the king had won and corrupted with money) did make unto them. Whereupon Manius dispatched ambassadors unto the cities, and sent Titus Quintius Flamininus among others, who kept the greatest part of the people from rebelling (that were easily drawn to give ear to this innovation) as we have expressed more amply in his *Life*: and Cato being sent [as an] ambassador also, persuaded the Corinthians, those of Patras, and the Ægians, and made them stick still to the Romans, and continued a long time at Athens. Some say they find an oration of his written in the Greek tongue, which he made before the Athenians, in commendation of their ancestors: wherein he said, he took great pleasure to see Athens, for the beauty and stateliness of the city. But this is false.

Now King Antiochus kept all the straits and narrow passages of the mountains called Thermopyles [*Thermopylae*], (being the ordinary way and entry into Greece) and had fortified them as well with his army that camped at the foot of the mountain, as also with walls and trenches he had made by hand, besides the natural strength and fortification of the mount itself in sundry places: and so he determined to remain there, trusting to his own strength and fortifications aforesaid, and to turn the force of the wars some other way. The Romans also, they despaired utterly they should be able any way to charge him before. But Cato remembering with himself **the** compass [and circuit] the Persians had fetched about before time likewise to enter into Greece: he departed one night from the camp with part of the army: to prove if he could find the very compass about, the barbarous people had made before.

But as they climbed up the mountain, their guide that was one of the prisoners taken in the country, lost his way, and made them wander up and down in marvellous steep rocks and crooked ways, that the poor soldiers were in marvellous ill taking. Cato seeing the danger they were brought into by this **lewd** guide, commanded all his soldiers not to stir a foot from thence, and **to tarry him there**: and in the meantime he went himself alone, and Lucius Manlius with him (a lusty man, and nimble to climb upon the rocks) and so went forward at adventure, taking extreme and incredible pain, and in as much danger of his life, grubbing all night in the dark without moonlight, through wild olive trees, and high rocks, [there being nothing but precipices and darkness before their eyes], until they stumbled at the length upon a little pathway, which went as they thought directly to the foot of the mountain, where the camp of the enemies lay. So they set up certain marks and tokens, upon the highest tops of the rocks they could choose, by view of eye to be discerned furthest upon the mountain called Callidromus. And when they had done that, they returned back again to fetch the soldiers, whom they led towards their marks they had set up: until at the length they found their pathway again, where they put their soldiers in order to march.

Narration and Discussion

How does Plutarch say that Cato was different from most people who held high office? Did Cato show humility or greed (ambition) by his willingness to take on post-consul challenges?

Tell the events of this adventure so far. What do you think will happen next?

Lesson Seven

Introduction

The adventure continues!

Vocabulary

at a trice: instantly

after what sort: in what way

advertised: informed

straits: narrow places

press: crowd or mass of people

holden in: hemmed in

ostentation: showing off

incontinently: quickly

Reading

Now they went not far in this path they found, but the way failed them straight, and brought them to a bog: but then they were in worse case than before, and in greater fear, not knowing they were so near their enemies, as indeed they were. The day began to break a little, and one of them that marched foremost, thought he heard a noise, and that he saw the Greeks' camp at the foot of the rocks, and certain soldiers that kept watch there. Whereupon Cato made them stay, and willed only the Firmanians to come unto him, and none but them, because he had found them faithful before, and very ready to obey his commandment. They were with him **at a trice** to know his pleasure: so Cato said unto them: My fellows, I must have some of our enemies taken prisoners, that I may know of them who they be that keep that passage, what number they be, what order they keep, how they are camped and armed, and **after what sort** they determine to fight with us. The way to work this feat, standeth upon swiftness, and hardiness to run upon them suddenly, as lions do, which which being naked fear not to run into the midst of any herd of fearful beasts.

    He had no sooner spoken these words, but the Firmanian soldiers began to run down the mountain, as they were, upon those that kept the watch: and so setting upon them, they being out of order, made them fly, and took an armed man prisoner. When they had him, they straight brought him unto Cato, who by the prisoner was **advertised**, how that the strength of their enemies' army was lodged about the person of the king, within the straight and valley of the said mountain: and that the soldiers they saw, were six hundred Ætolians, all brave soldiers, whom they had chosen and appointed to keep the top of the rocks over King Antiochus's camp.

When Cato had heard him, making small account of the matter, as well for their small number, as also for the ill order they kept: he made the trumpets sound straight, and his soldiers to march in battle with great cries, himself being the foremost man of all his troop, with a sword drawn in his hand. But when the Ætolians saw them coming down the rocks towards them, they began to fly for life unto their great camp, which they filled full of fear, trouble, and all disorder.

Now Manlius at the same present also, gave an assault unto the walls and fortifications the king had made, overthwart the valleys and **straits** of the mountains: at which assault, King Antiochus [him]self had a blow on the face with a stone, that strake some of his teeth out of his mouth, so that for very pain and anguish he felt, he turned his horse back, and got him behind the **press**.

And then there were none of his army that made any more resistance, or that could abide the fierceness of the Romans. But notwithstanding that the places were very ill for flying, because it was unpossible for them to scatter and straggle, being **holden in** with high rocks on the one side of them, and with bogs and deep marshes on the other side, which they must needs fall into if their feet slipped, or were thrust forward by any: yet they fell one upon another in the straits, and ran so in heaps together, that they cast themselves away, for fear of the Romans' swords that lighted upon them in every corner.

And there Marcus Cato, that never made ceremony or niceness to praise himself openly [*meaning he did praise himself*], nor reckoned it any shame to do it: did take a present occasion for it, as falleth out upon all victory and famous exploits. And so did set it out with all the **ostentation** and brave words he could give. For he wrote with his own hands, that such as saw him chase and lay upon his flying enemies that day, were driven to say, that Cato was not bound to the Romans, but the Romans bound unto Cato. And then Manius the Consul [him]self, being in a great heat with the fury of the battle, embraced Cato a great while, that was also hot with chasing of the enemy: and spake aloud with great joy before them all, that neither he, nor the people of Rome could recompense Cato for his valiant service that day.

After this battle, the Consul Manius sent Cato to Rome, to be the messenger himself to report the news of the victory. So he embarked **incontinently**, and had such a fair wind, that he passed over the sea to Brindes [*Brundusium*] without any danger, and victory; went from thence unto Tarentum in one day, and from Tarentum in four days more to Rome. And so he came to Rome in five days after his landing in Italy, and made such speed, that himself was indeed the first messenger that brought news of the victory. Whereupon he filled all Rome with joy and sacrifices, and made the Romans so proud, that ever after they thought themselves able men to conquer the world both by sea and land. And these be all the martial deeds and noble acts Cato did.

Narration and Discussion

Do you think Cato's own account of his bravery was accurate? Why or why not?

Lesson Eight

Introduction

Cato stayed busy in public life, eventually deciding to run for censor.

Vocabulary

>**sued to be censor:** ran for that office
>
>**patrician:** of a noble family
>
>**keep books of them:** keep account of them
>
>**prerogatives:** privileges
>
>**shewing no countenance:** giving no indication

meale mouthed: mealy-mouthed; insincere

as if he had been present officer, and no suitor for the office: as if he had already held the office of censor and not just been running for it

prince of the Senate: head man in the Senate

to take it clean away, and to be openly seen in it: to outlaw the feasting and luxuries altogether, and to take personal responsibility for that action

prodigality: spending money on luxuries

Cato was envied: Dryden translates this as "those who were disgusted at Cato."

superfluous: extra, unnecessary

marry: an exclamation of surprise or emphasis

Reading

Marcus Cato, ten years after his Consulship, **sued to be censor**, which was in Rome the greatest office of dignity that any citizen of Rome could attain unto: and as a man may say, the room of all glory and honour in their commonwealth. For among other authorities the censor had power to examine men's lives and manners, and to punish every offender. For the Romans were of that mind, that they would not have men marry, get children, live privately by themselves, and make feasts and banquets at their pleasure, but that they should stand in fear to be reproved and inquired of by the magistrate: and that it was not good to give everybody liberty, to do what they would, following his own lust and fancy. And they judging that men's natural dispositions do appear more in such things, than in all other things that are openly done at noondays, and in the sight of the world: used to choose two censors, that were two surveyors of manners, to see that every man behaved himself virtuously, and gave not themselves to pleasure, nor to break the laws and customs of the commonwealth.

These officers were called in their tongue, Censors, and always of custom one of them was a **patrician**, and the other a commoner. These two had power and authority to disgrade a knight by taking away his horse, and to put [*out*] any of the Senate, whom they saw live dissolutely and disorderly. It was their office also, to [assess] and rate every citizen according to the estimation of their goods, to note the age, genealogy and degrees of every man, and to **keep books of them**, besides many other **prerogatives** they had belonging to their office. Therefore when Cato came to sue for this office among other, the chiefest Senators were all bent against him, some of them for very envy. The Senators thinking it shame and dishonour to the nobility, to suffer men that were meanly born, and upstarts (the first of their house and name, that ever came to bear office in the state) to be called and preferred unto the highest offices of state in all their commonwealth. Other also that were ill livers, and knowing that they had offended the laws of their country: they feared his cruelty too much, imagining he would spare no man, nor pardon any offence, having the law in his own hands. So when they had consulted together about it, they did set up seven competitors against him, who flattered the people with many fair words and promises, as though they had need of magistrates to use them gently, and to do things for to please them.

But Cato contrariwise, **shewing no countenance** that he would use them gently in the office, but openly in the pulpit for orations, threatening those that had lived naughtily and wickedly, he cried out: that they must reform their city, and persuaded the people not to choose the gentlest, but the sharpest physicians: and that himself was such a one as they needed, and among the Patricians Valerius Flaccus another, in whose company he hoped (they two being chosen censors) to do great good unto the commonwealth, by burning and cutting of (like Hydra's heads) all vanity and voluptuous pleasures, that were crept in amongst them: and that he saw well enough, how all the other suitors sought the office by dishonest means, fearing such officers as they knew would deal justly and uprightly.

Then did the people of Rome shew themselves nobly minded, and worthy of noble governors. For they refused not the sourness or severity of Cato, but rejected these **meale mouthed** men, that seemed ready to please the people in all things: and thereupon chose Marcus Cato censor, and Valerius Flaccus to be his fellow, and they did obey him, **as if he had been present officer, and no suitor for**

the office, being in themselves to give it to whom they thought good.

The first thing he did after he was [in]stalled in his censorship, was: that he named Lucius Valerius Flaccus, his friend and fellow censor with him, **prince of the Senate**.

Cato put out of the Senate one Manilius, who was in great towardness to have been made consul the next year following, only because he kissed his wife too lovingly in the daytime, and before his daughter: and reproving him for it, he [Cato] told him, his wife never kissed him, but when it thundered. So when he was disposed to be merry, he would say it was happy with him when Jupiter thundered.

He took away Lucius Scipio's horse from him, that had triumphed for the victories he had won against the great King Antiochus: which won him much ill will, because it appeared to the world he did it of purpose, for the malice he did bear Scipio the African, that was dead. But the [worst] thing that grieved the people of all other extremities he used, was his putting down of all feasts and vain expenses. For a man **to take it clean away, and to be openly seen in it**, it was unpossible, because it was so common a thing, and every man was given so to it. Therefore Cato to fetch it about indirectly, did praise every citizen's goods, and rated [*assessed*] their apparel, their coaches, their litters, their wives' chains and jewels, and all other moveables and household stuff, that had cost above a thousand five hundred drachmas apiece, at ten times as much as they were worth: to the end that such as had bestowed their money in those curious trifles, should pay so much more subsidy to the maintenance of the commonwealth, as their goods were over-valued at. Moreover he ordained for every thousand asses [*coins: see previous note*] that those trifling things were praised at, the owners of them should pay three thousand asses to the common treasury: to the end that they who were grieved with this tax, and saw other pay less subsidy (that were as much worth as themselves, by living without such toys) might [be tired out of their **prodigality**].

Notwithstanding, **Cato was envied** every way. First, of them that were contented to pay the tax imposed, rather than they would leave their vanity: and next, of them also, that would rather reform themselves, than pay the tax. And some think that this law was devised rather to take away their goods, than to let them to make shew of them: and they have a fond opinion besides, that their riches

[are] better seen in **superfluous** things, than in necessary. Whereat they say Aristotle the Philosopher did wonder more, than at any other thing: how men could think them more rich and happy, that had many curious and superfluous things, than those that had necessary and profitable things. And Scopas the Thessalian, when one of his familiar friends asked him, I know not what trifling thing, and to make him grant it the sooner, told him it was a thing he might well spare, and did him no good: **marry** sayeth he, all the goods I have, are in such toys as do me no good. So this covetous desire we have to be rich, cometh of no necessary desire in nature, but is bred in us by a false opinion from the common sort.

Narration and Discussion

How did Cato try to make the people of Rome a little less fond of their material goods? Was it successful? Can you think of any similar examples of a "luxury tax" now? Does it work?

Lesson Nine

Introduction

Popular or unpopular? Right or wrong? Is what was good for the city good for Cato's reputation? Did it matter?

Vocabulary

- **and moreover raised the common farms and customs of the city, as high as he could:** Dryden translates it this way: "He beat down also the price in contracts for public works to the lowest, and raised it in contracts for farming the taxes to the highest sum." Even that phrasing is a bit confusing! Let's just put it that Cato arranged for some public building work to be done at a low rate; and he made himself unpopular with those who were profiting at public expense.
- **tribunes of the people:** those who represented the common people in the Senate
- **diverse mean men and unknown persons:** insignificant people

about the time his wife did unswaddle the young boy to wash and shift him: he liked to be home for the baby's bath time

Reading

Now, Cato caring least of all for the exclamations they made against him, grew to be more straight and severe. For he cut off the pipes and quills private men had made to convey water into their houses and gardens, robbing the city of the water that came from their common conduit heads, and did pluck down also men's porches that were made before their doors into the street, and brought down the praises of common workers in the city, **and moreover raised the common farms and customs of the city, as high as he could**: all which things together made him greatly hated and envied of most men. Wherefore, Titus Flamininus, and certain other[s] being bent against him in open Senate, caused all Cato's covenants and bargains made with the master workmen, for repairing and mending of the common buildings and holy places, to be made void, as things greatly prejudicial to the commonwealth. And they did also stir up the boldest and rashest of the **tribunes of the people** against him, because they should accuse him unto the people, and make request he might be condemned in the sum of two talents. They did marvellously hinder also the building of the palace he built at the charge of the commonwealth, looking into the marketplace [*the Forum*] under the Senate house: which palace was finished notwithstanding, and called after his name. Basilica Porcia: as who would say, the palace Porcius built.

Howbeit it seemed the people of Rome did greatly like and commend his government in the censorship. For they set up a statue of him in the temple of the goddess of health, whereunder they wrote not his victories nor triumph, but only engraved this inscription word for word, to this effect by translation:

> For the honour of Marcus Cato the Censor: because
> he reformed the discipline of the commonwealth of
> Rome (that was far out of order, and given to
> licentious life) by his wise precepts, good manners,
> and holy institutions.

Indeed, before this image was set up for him, he was wont to mock at them that delighted, and were desirous of such things:

saying, they did not consider how Honour they bragged in [was that of brass-]founders, painters, and image makers, but changeth nothing of their virtues: and that for himself, the people [themselves] did always carry lively images of him in their hearts, meaning the memory of his life and doings. When some wondered why **diverse mean men and unknown persons** had images set up of them, and there were none of him: he gave them this answer: I had rather men should ask why Cato had no image set up for him, than why he had any.

In the end, he would have no honest man abide to be praised, unless his praise turned to the benefit of the commonwealth: and yet was he one of them that would most praise himself. So that if any had done a fault, or stepped awry, and that men had gone about to reprove them: he would say they were not to be blamed, for they were no Catos that did offend. And such as counterfeited to follow any of his doings, and came short of his manner, he called them left-hand Catos. He would say, that in most dangerous times the Senate used to cast their eyes upon him, as passengers on the sea do look upon the master of the ship in a storm: and that many times when he was absent, the Senate would put over matters of importance, until he might come among them. And this is confirmed to be true, as well by other, as by himself. His authority was great in matters of state, for his wisdom, his eloquence, and great experience.

Besides this commendation, they praised him for a good father to his children, a good husband to his wife, and a good saver for his profit: for he was never careless of them, as things to be lightly passed on. And therefore methinks I must needs tell you by the way, some part of his well doing, to follow our declaration of him. First of all, he married a gentlewoman more noble than rich, knowing that either of both should make her proud and stout enough: but yet he ever thought the nobler born, would be the more ashamed of dishonesty, than the meaner born: and therefore that they would be more obedient to their husbands, in all honest manner and reasonable things. Furthermore, he said: that he that beat his wife or his child, did commit as great a sacrilege, as if he polluted or spoiled the holiest things of the world: and he thought it a greater praise for a man to be a good husband, than a good Senator. And therefore he thought nothing more commendable in the life of old Socrates, than his patience, in using his wife well, that was such a shrew, and his children that were so harebrained.

After Cato's wife had brought him a son, he could not have so earnest business in hand, if it had not touched the commonwealth, but he would let all alone, to go home to his house, **about the time his wife did unswaddle the young boy to wash and shift him**. When his son was come to age of discretion, and that he was able to learn any thing, Cato himself did teach him, notwithstanding he had a slave in his house called Chilo (a very honest man, and a good grammarian) who did also teach many other: but as he said himself, he did not like, a slave should rebuke his grammarian, nor pull him by the ears, when peradventure he was not apt to take very suddenly that was taught him: neither would he have his son bound to a slave for so great a matter as that, as to have his learning of him. Wherefore he himself taught him his grammar, the law, and to exercise his body, not only to throw a dart, to play at the sword, to ride a horse, and to handle all sorts of weapons, but also to fight with fists, to abide cold and heat, and to swim over a swift running river. He said moreover, that he wrote goodly histories in great letters with his own hand, because his son might learn in his father's house virtues of good men in times past, that he taking example their doings, should frame his life to excel them. He also, that he took as great heed of speaking any uncomely words before his son, as he would have done if he had been before the Vestal Nuns.

[When he grew up], this Cato [the son] married Tertia, one of Paulus Æmilius's daughters, and sister unto Scipio the second, and so was matched in this noble house, not only for his own virtue's sake, but for respect of his father's dignity and authority: whereby the great care, pains, and study that Cato the father took in bringing up his son in virtue and learning, was honourably rewarded in the happy bestowing of his son.

Narration and Discussion

Explain the following: "... he would have no honest man abide to be praised, unless his praise turned to the benefit of the commonwealth: and yet was he one of them that would most praise himself."

"Howbeit it seemed the people of Rome did greatly like and commend his government in the Censorship." Why do you think this was so?

Whom did Cato call "left-hand Catos?"

Why did Cato take on the education of his son himself? Would you like to have had him for a teacher?

Lesson Ten

Introduction

As mentioned previously, Cato had strange ideas about slaves; he also had some questionable ways of making money, and these are described in Part One of this lesson. Part Two is about the latest fad to hit Rome: Greek philosophy.

Vocabulary

tractable: easy to rule

usury: the practice of making unethical or immoral monetary loans intended to unfairly enrich the lender

factor: agent

manumised: freed

And thus he did not venture all the money he lent, but a little piece only for his part, and got marvellous riches by his usury: Dryden translates this, "so that there was no danger of losing his whole stock, but only a little part, and that with a prospect of great profit."

Stoic: a follower of Stoicism, a school of Greek philosophy

had no dispatch: had no real business to conduct

a busy man, and a stirrer up of sedition: a busybody and a troublemaker

Reading

Part One

[Cato] ever had a great number of young little slaves which he bought, when any would sell their prisoners in the wars. He did choose them thus young, because they were apt yet to learn any thing he would train them unto, and that a man might break them, like young colts, or little whelps. But none of them all, how many soever he had, did ever go to any man's house, but when himself or his wife did send them. If any man asked them what Cato did: they answered, they could not tell. And when they were within, either they must needs be occupied about somewhat, or else they must sleep: for he loved them well that were sleepy, holding opinion that slaves that loved sleep were more **tractable**, and willing to do any thing a man would set them to, than those that were waking.

 At the first when he gave himself to follow the wars, and was not greatly rich, he never was angry for any fault his servants did about his person: saying it was a foul thing for a gentleman or noble man, to fall out with his servants for his belly. Afterwards, as he rose to better state, and grew to be wealthy, if he had made a dinner or supper for any of his friends and familiars, and they were no sooner gone, but he would scourge them with whips and leather thongs, that had not waited as they should have done at the board, or had forgotten any thing he would have had done. He would ever craftily make one of them fall out with another: for he could not abide they should be friends, being ever jealous of that. If any of them had done a fault that deserved death, he would declare his offence before them all: and then if they condemned him to die, he would put him to death before them all.

 Howbeit in his latter time he grew greedy, and gave up his tillage, saying it was rather pleasant, than profitable. Therefore because he would lay out his money surely, and bring a certain revenue to his purse, he bestowed it upon ponds, natural hot baths, places fit for fullers' craft, upon meadows and pastures, upon coppices and young wood: and of all these; he made a great and a more quiet revenue yearly, which he would say, Jupiter himself could not diminish. Furthermore, he was a great **usurer**, both by land and by sea: and the **usury** he took by sea was most extreme of all other, for he used it in this sort. He would have them to whom he lent his money unto, that trafficked by sea, to have many partners, and to the number of fifty: and that they should have so many ships. Then he would venture among them for a part only [*i.e. he bought one share*], whereof Quintius his slave whom he had **manumised**, was made his **factor**, and [Quintius] used to sail, and trafficked with the merchants, to whom he had lent his money out to usury. **And thus he did not venture all the money he lent, but a little piece only for his part, and got marvellous riches by his usury.**

Part Two

Furthermore, when Cato was grown very old, Carneades the Academic, and Diogenes the **Stoic**, were sent from Athens as ambassadors to Rome, to sue for a release of a fine of five hundred talents which they had imposed on the Athenians upon a condemnation passed against them, for a contempt of appearance, by the sentence of the Sicyonians, at the suit of the Oropians. [*The Athenians had not shown up for a court appearance and were being fined for it.*]

Immediately when these two philosophers were arrived in the city of Rome, the young gentlemen that were given to their books, did visit and welcome them, and gave great reverence to them after they had heard them speak, and specially to Carneades: whose grace in speaking, and force of persuading was no less, than the fame ran upon him, and specially when he was to speak in so great an audience, and before such a state, as would not suppress his praise. Rome straight was full, as if a wind had blown this rumor into every man's ear: that there was a Grecian arrived, a famous learned man, who with his eloquence would lead a man as he lust. There was no other talk awhile through the whole city, he had so inflamed the young gentlemen's minds with love and desire to be learned: that all other pleasures and delights were set aside, and they disposed themselves to no other exercise, but to the study of Philosophy, as if some secret and divine inspiration from above had procured them to it. Whereof the Lords and Senators of Rome were glad, and rejoiced much to see their youth so well given to knowledge, and to the study of the Greek tongue, and to delight in the company of these two great and excellent learned men. But Marcus Cato, even from the beginning that young men began to study the Greek tongue, and that it grew in estimation in Rome, did dislike of it: fearing least the youth of Rome that were desirous of learning and eloquence, would utterly give over the honour and glory of arms.

Furthermore, when he saw the estimation and fame of these two personages did increase more and more, and in such sort that Caius Aquilius, one of the chiefest of the Senate, made suit to be their interpreter: he determined then to convey them out of the city by some [pretence]. So he openly found fault one day in the Senate, that the ambassadors were long there, and **had no dispatch**: considering also they were cunning men, and could easily persuade what they would. And if there were no other respect, this only might persuade them to determine some answer for them, and so to send them home again to their schools, to teach their children of Greece, and to let alone the children of Rome, that they might learn to obey the laws and the Senate, as they had done before.

Now he spake this to the Senate, not of any private ill will or malice he bare to Carneades, as some men thought: but because he generally hated philosophy, and of an ambition despised the muses, and knowledge of the Greek tongue. Which was the more suspected, because he had said, the ancient Socrates was but **a busy man, and a stirrer up of sedition**, and sought by all means possible to usurp tyranny, and rule in his country: by perverting and changing the manners and customs of the same, and alluring the subjects thereof to a disliking of their laws and ancient customs. And he laughed at Isocrates' school, that taught the art of eloquence: saying, his scholars waxed old, and were still so long a-learning, that they meant to use their eloquence and plead causes in another world, before Minos, when they were dead. Therefore, to pluck his son from the study of the Greek tongue, he said to him with a strained voice, and in a bigger sound than he was wont to do: (as if he had spoken to him by way of prophecy or inspiration) that so long as the Romans disposed themselves to study the Greek tongue, so long would they mar and bring all to nought.

And yet time hath proved his vain words false and untrue, for the city of Rome did never flourish so much, nor the Roman Empire was ever so great, as at that time, when learning and the Greek tongue most flourished.

Narration and Discussion

"Slaves that loved sleep were more tractable, and willing to do any thing a man would set them to, than those that were waking." Is there a warning there for us about too much sleep? (Proverbs 6:10-11)

Explain Cato's financial strategy, using his former slave as an agent. Was it honest?

Why was Cato so concerned to see the young people caught up in the new fad of Greek philosophy? Does this seem to contradict what Plutarch wrote about him earlier? "They say he fell in his very old age to the study of the Greek tongue, and to read Greek books, and that he profited somewhat by Thucydides, but much more by Demosthenes, to frame his matter, and also to be eloquent. Which plainly appeareth, in all his books and writings, full of authorities, examples, and stories taken out of Greek authors: and many of his sentences and morals, his adages and quick answers, are translated out of the same word for word."

Lesson Eleven

Introduction

At the end of his life, Cato had two pet peeves: philosophers and physicians. But that didn't stop him from writing his own health book . . . and a farming book . . . and sharing his recipe for tarts.

Vocabulary

physic: medicine

saving that: except that

husbandry: farm

Reading

Howbeit Cato did not only hate the philosophers of Greece, but did dislike them also, that professed **physic** in Rome. For he had either heard or read the answer Hippocrates made, when the king of Persia sent for him, and offered him a great sum of gold and silver, if he would come and serve him: who sware he would never serve the barbarous people, that were natural enemies to the Grecians. So Cato affirmed, it was an oath that all other physicians sware ever after: wherefore he commanded his son to fly from them all alike, and said he had written a little book of physic, the which he did heal those of his house when they were sick, and did keep them in health when they were whole. He never forbade them to eat, but did always bring them up with herbs, and certain light meats, as mallard, ringdoves, and hares: for such meats, said he, are good for the sick, and light of digestion, **saving that** they make them [dream a little too much]. He boasted also how with this manner of physic, he did always keep himself in health, and his family from sickness.

Yet for all that, I take it, he did not all that he bragged of: for he buried both his wife, and his son also. But he himself was of a strong nature, and a lusty body, full of strength, and health, and lived long without sickness: so that when he was a very old man and past marriage, he loved women well, and married a young maiden for that cause only.

Cato had a son by his second wife, whom he named after her name, Cato Salonian: and his eldest son died in his office being praetor, of whom he often speaketh in divers of his books, commending him for a very honest man. And they say, he took the death of him very patiently, and like a grave wise man, not leaving therefore to do any service or business for the state, otherwise than he did before.

And therein he did not, as Lucius Lucullus, and Metellus surnamed Pius, did afterwards: who gave up meddling any more with matters of government and state, after they were waxen old. For he thought it a charge and duty, whereunto every honest man whilst he lived, was bound in all piety. Nor as Scipio African had done before him, who perceiving that the glory and fame of his doings did purchase him the ill will of the citizens, he changed the rest of his life into quietness, and forsook the city and all dealings in commonwealth, and went and dwelt in the country.

But as there was one that told Dionysius, the tyrant of Syracuse, as it is written, that he could not die more honourably, than to be buried in the tyranny: even so did Cato think, that he could not wax more honestly old, than in serving of the commonwealth, unto his dying day. So at vacant times, when Cato was desirous a little to recreate and refresh himself, he passed his time away in making of books, and looking upon his **husbandry** in the country. This is the cause why he wrote so many kinds of books and stories. But his tillage and husbandry in the country, he did tend and follow all in his youth, for his profit. For he said he had but two sorts of revenue, tillage, and sparing: but in age, whatsoever he did in the country, it was all for pleasure, and to learn something ever of nature. For he hath written a book of the country life, and of tillage, in the which he sheweth how to make tarts and cakes, and how to keep fruits. He would needs shew such singularity and skill in all things: when he was in his house in the country, he fared a little better than he did in other places, and would oftentimes bid his neighbours, and such as had land lying about him, to come and sup with him, and he would be merry with them: so that his company was not only pleasant, and liking to old folks as himself, but also to the younger sort. For he had seen much, and had experience in many things, and used much pleasant talk, profitable for the hearers. He thought the board one of the chiefest means to breed love amongst men, and at his own table would always praise good men and virtuous citizens, but would suffer no talk of evil men, neither in their praise nor dispraise.

Narration and Discussion

What do you think of Cato's health plan? Did it seem to work well? (Look back at Lesson Nine and see where his statue was erected. Was this appropriate?)

Lesson Twelve

Introduction

Near the end of his life, Cato had a warning and some advice for the

Roman government: the city of Carthage was stronger than ever, and it was likely that they would start a war with Rome, or at least prove to be a dangerous enemy. He turned out to be right.

Vocabulary

razed it utterly: brought it to the ground

Carthage carried a high sail, and stopped not for a little: Carthage was doing well, "riding high"

to leave to understand: stop worrying about

insolency: lack of respect for authority, or (in this case) overconfidence in themselves, lack of humility

Reading

Now it is thought the last notable act and service he did in the commonwealth, was the overthrow of Carthage: for indeed he that won it, and **razed it utterly**, was Scipio the second, but it was chiefly through Cato's counsel and advice, that the last war was taken in hand against the Carthaginians, and it of the last chanced upon this occasion.

Cato was sent into Africa to understand the cause and controversy that was between the Carthaginians and Massinissa, king of Numidia, which were at great wars together. And he was sent thither, because king Massinissa had ever been a friend unto the Romans, and for that the Carthaginians were become their confederates since the last wars, in the which they were overthrown by Scipio the first, who took for a fine of them, a great part of their Empire, and imposed upon them besides, a great yearly tribute.

Now when he was come into that country, he found not the city of Carthage in misery, beggary, and out of heart, as the Romans supposed: but full of lusty youths very rich and wealthy, and great store of armour and munition in it for the wars, so that by reason of the wealth thereof, **Carthage carried a high sail, and stopped not for a little.** Wherefore he thought that it was more than time for the Romans **to leave to understand** the controversies betwixt the Carthaginians and Massinissa, and rather to provide betimes to destroy Carthage, that had been ever an ancient enemy to the Romans, and ever sought to be revenged of that they had suffered at their hands before, and that they were now grown to that greatness and courage in so short time, as in manner it was incredible: so as it was likely they would fall into as great enmity with the Romans, as they ever did before.

Therefore so soon as he returned to Rome, he plainly told the Senate, that the losses and harms the Carthaginians had received by the last wars they had with them, had not so much diminished their power and strength, as the same had shewed their own folly and lack of wisdom: for it was to be feared much, least their late troubles had made them more skilful, than weakened them for the wars.

And that they made wars now with the Numidians, to exercise them only, meaning afterwards to war with themselves [*Rome*]: and that the peace they had made with them, was but an intermission and stay of wars, only expecting time and opportunity to break with them again. They say moreover, that besides the persuasions he used, he brought with him of purpose, African figs in his long sleeves, which he shook out amongst them in the Senate. When the Senators marvelled to see so goodly fair green figs, he said: The country that beareth them, is not above three days' sailing from Rome.

But yet this is more strange which they report of him besides: that he never declared his opinion in any matter in the Senate after that, but this was ever the one end of his tale: Methinketh still Carthage would be utterly destroyed.

Publius Scipio Nasica, used ever in like manner the contrary speech: that he thought it meet Carthage should stand. Scipio saw, in my opinion, that the Romans through their pride and insolency were full of absurdities, and carried themselves very high, by reason of their happy success and victories, and were so lofty minded, that the Senate could hardly rule them: and that by reason of their great authority, they imagined they might bring their city to what height they would. Therefore he spake it, that the fear of Carthage might always continue as a bridle, to reign in the **insolency** of the people of Rome, who knew well enough, that the Carthaginians were of no sufficient power to make wars with the Romans, nor yet to overcome them: and even so were they not wholly to be despised, and not to be feared at all.

Cato still replied to the contrary, that therein consisted the greatest danger of all: that a city which was ever of great force and power, and had been punished by former wars and misery, would always have an eye of revenge to their enemies, and be much like a horse that had broken his halter, that being unbridled, would run upon his rider. And therefore he thought it not good, nor sound advice, so to suffer the Carthaginians to recover their strength, but rather they ought altogether to take away all outward danger, and the fear they stood in to lose their conquest: and specially, when they left means within the city [it]self to fall still again to their former rebellion. And this is the cause why they suppose Cato was the occasion of the third and last war the Romans had against the Carthaginians.

But now when the war was begun, Cato died, and before his death he prophesied, as a man would say, who it should be that should end those wars. And it was Scipio the second, who being a young man at that time, had charge only as a colonel over a thousand footmen: but in all battles, and wheresoever there was wars, he shewed himself ever valiant and wise. Insomuch as news being brought thereof continually unto Rome, and Cato hearing them, spake as they say, these two verses of Homer:

> This only man right wise, reputed is to be,
> all other seem but shadows set, by such wise men as he.

Which prophecy, Scipio soon after confirmed true by his doings.

Moreover, the issue Cato left behind him, was a son he had by his second wife: who was called (as we said before) Cato Salonian, by reason of his mother, and a little boy of his eldest son that died before him. This Cato Salonian died being praetor, but he left a son behind him that came to be consul, and was grandfather unto Cato the Philosopher, one of the most virtuous men of his time.

Narration and Discussion

How did Cato become so involved, in his old age, with the question of Carthage? What were the fresh figs intended to demonstrate?

Cato quotes some lines from Homer, referring to Scipio. Do they apply as well to himself?

Notes

1. Miss R.A. Pennethorne, "P.N.E.U. Principles As Illustrated by Teaching," *The Parents' Review*, 10 (1899): 549, AmblesideOnline. http://www.amblesideonline.org/PR/PR10p549PNEUPrinciples.shtml

Philopoemen

"Philopoemen, Prince of the Achaeans…is commended because in time of peace he never had anything in his mind but the rules of war; and when he was in the country with friends, he often stopped and reasoned with them: 'If the enemy should be upon that hill, and we should find ourselves here with our army, with whom would be the advantage? How should one best advance to meet him, keeping the ranks? If we should wish to retreat, how ought we to pursue?' And he would set forth to them, as he went, all the chances that could befall an army; he would listen to their opinion and state his, confirming it with reasons, so that by these continual discussions there could never arise, in time of war, any unexpected circumstances that he could not deal with." Niccolo Machiavelli, *The Prince* (1532)

Introduction

Philopoemen (Phila-PEE-men) lived from 253 to 184 B.C. (*Plutarch says 183 B.C.*), during the last days of ancient Greece, when Rome was flourishing but the Greek city-states had lost much of their power. Philopoemen's home was Megalopolis, which means "big city," similar to "Metropolis." Megalopolis was located in Arcadia, which is in the Peloponnese—the southern part of Greece that looks almost like a large island. North spells the name of the people who lived there "Megalipolitans."

Notes on Spelling

There are at least two English spellings: Philopoemen and Philopoemon. I've also seen it spelled Philopoimen. This can be helpful for online searches.

Achaia was a territory on the northern coast of the Peloponnese; and the Achaian League was a confederation of Greek city-states in that area. Achaia (North's spelling) can also be spelled Achaea (Dryden's preference).

Lesson One

Introduction

Philopoemen was brought up and educated by his father's friend Cassander, and by two other excellent tutors. Plutarch's list of the tutors' other achievements is not important for our purposes; the point is that, after all these other things, they still considered their education of Philopoemen to be "among their best actions." To show why this is so is one of Plutarch's aims in writing this *Life*.

Vocabulary

> **to requite the love**: to pay back or honour the friendship
>
> **to grow to man's estate**: to grow past the childhood years
>
> **took him into their government:** took over his education
>
> **he went plainly:** he dressed plainly
>
> **to inn there all night:** to stay there for the night
>
> **began to fall to hew wood:** began to chop wood
>
> **riving of wood:** chopping wood

Reading

In the city of Mantinea, there was a citizen in old time called Cassander, one that was as nobly born and of as great authority in government there, as any man of his time whatsoever. Notwithstanding, fortune frowned on him in the end, insomuch as he was driven out of his country, and went to live in the city of Megalopolis, only for the love he bare unto Crausis, Philopoemen's father, a rare man, and nobly given in all things, and one that loved him also very well. Now so long as Crausis lived, Cassander was so well used at his hands, that he could lack nothing: and when he was departed this world, Cassander, to **requite the love** Crausis bare him in his lifetime, took his son into his charge, being an orphan, and Cassander taught him, as Homer's Achilles was brought up by the old Phoenix. So this child Philopoemen grew to have noble conditions, and increased always from good to better.

Afterwards, when he came **to grow to man's [e]state**, Ecdemus and Demophanes, both Megalipolitans, **took him into their government**. They were two philosophers that had been hearers of Arcesilaus, in the school of Academia, and afterwards employed all the philosophy they had learned, upon the governing of the commonwealth, and dealing in matters of state, as much or more than any other men of their time. For they delivered their city from the tyranny of Aristodemus, who kept it in subjection, [and whom they caused to be killed]. And they did help Aratus also to drive the tyrant Niocles, out of Sicyone [*see note on Aratus in Lesson Five*]. At the request of the Cyrenians, that were troubled with civil dissension and factions among them, they went unto Cyrena, where they did reform the state of the commonwealth, and [e]stablished good laws for them. But for themselves, they reckoned the education and bringing up of Philopoemen, the chiefest act that ever they did: judging that they had procured a universal good unto all Greece, to bring up a man of so noble a nature, in the rules and precepts of philosophy.

And to say truly, Greece did love him passingly well, as the last valiant man she brought forth in her [old] age, after so many great and famous ancient captains: and did always increase his power and authority, as his glory did also rise. Whereupon there was a Roman, who to praise him the more, called him the last of the Grecians: that after him, Greece never brought forth any worthy person, deserving the name of a Grecian. And now concerning his person, he had no ill face, as many suppose he had: for his whole image is yet to be seen in the city of Delphi, excellently well done, as if he were alive.

And for that they report of his hostess in the city of Megara, who took him for a serving man: that was by reason of his courtesy, not standing upon his reputation, and because **he went plainly** besides. For she understanding that the general of the Achaians came **to inn there all night**, she bestirred her, and was very busy preparing for his supper, her husband peradventure being from home at that time: and in the mean season came Philopoemen into the inn, with a poor cloak on his back. The simple woman seeing him no better appareled, took him for one of his men that came before to provide his lodging, and so prayed him to lend her his hand in the kitchen. He straight cast off his cloak, and began to fall **to hew wood**. So, as Philopoemen was busy about it, in cometh her husband, and finding him **riving of wood**: Ha ha ha he, my Lord Philopoemen, why what meaneth this? Truly nothing else, he [said] in his Dorican tongue, but that I am punished, because I am neither fair boy, nor goodly man.

It is true that Titus Quintius Flamininus said one day unto him, seeming to mock him for his personage: O Philopoemen, thou hast fair hands, and good legs, but thou hast no belly, for he was fine in the waist, and small-bodied. Notwithstanding, I take it this jesting tended rather to the proportion of his army, than of his body: because he had both good horsemen, and footmen, but he was often without money to pay them. [These are common anecdotes told of Philopoemen.]

Discussion and Narration

What can you tell so far about how the Greeks viewed Philopoemen, and how he viewed himself?

What did Titus Flamininus probably mean by saying Philopoemen had no belly?

Consider the value of being educated by the best statesmen, philosophers and theologians. How can we also enjoy such an education?

Lesson Two

Introduction

Everything Philopoemen did was concentrated towards one goal: being a great general. The books he read, the outdoor work he did, the way he spent his time—all were aimed only at his long-term plan. Although he was a talented wrestler, he decided that even athletic training conflicted with his military goals, so he gave that up. We begin to get a clear picture of who Philopoemen wanted to be, and where he wanted his life to go.

Vocabulary

> **heat and willfulness:** Dryden translates this "personal rivalry and resentment"
>
> **Epaminondas**: a Theban general and statesman of the 4th century B.C.; the founder of Megalopolis
>
> **to enterprise any thing:** to try or dare anything
>
> **choler:** temper
>
> **martial:** military
>
> **if they did surfeit:** if they overdid it
>
> **the foremost to go out, and the hindermost to come in:** the first one out and the last one in
>
> **tillage:** farming
>
> **gests:** tales of adventure
>
> **peradventure:** perhaps

Reading

But now to descend to his nature and conditions: it seemeth that the ambition and desire he had to win honour in his doings, was not without some **heat and willfulness**. For, because he would altogether follow **Epaminondas'** steps, he shewed his hardiness **to enterprise any thing**, his wisdom to execute all great matters, and his integrity also, in that no money could corrupt him: but in civil matters and controversies, he could hardly otherwhiles keep himself within the bonds of modesty, patience, and courtesy, but would often burst out into **choler**, and willfulness [unlike Epaminondas]. Wherefore it seemeth, that he was a better captain for wars, than a wise governor for peace.

And indeed, even from his youth he ever loved soldiers, and arms, and delighted marvellously in all martial exercises: as in handling of his weapon well, riding of horses gallantly, and in [vaulting] nimbly. And because he seemed to have a natural gift in wrestling, certain of his friends, and such as were careful of him, did wish him to give himself most unto that exercise. Then he asked them, if their life that made such profession, would be no hindrance to their **martial** exercises. Answer was made him again, that the disposition of the person, and manner of life that wrestlers used, and such as followed like exercises, was altogether contrary to the life and discipline of a soldier, and specially touching life and limb. For wrestlers studied altogether to keep themselves in good plight, by much sleeping, eating, and drinking, by labouring, and taking their ease at certain hours, by not missing a jot of their exercises: and besides, were in hazard to lose the force and strength of their body, **if they did surfeit** never so little, or passed their ordinary course and rule of diet. Where soldiers contrariwise are used to all change, and diversity of life, and specially be taught from their youth, to [endure] all hardness, and scarcity, and to watch in the night without sleep. Philopoemen hearing this, did not only forsake those exercises, and scorned them, but afterwards being general of an army, he sought by all infamous means he could to put down all wrestling, and such kind of exercise, which made men's bodies unmeet to make pains, and to become soldiers for to fight in defence of their country, that otherwise would have been very able and handsome for the same.

When he first left his book and schoolmasters, and began to wear armour in invasions the Mantineians used to make upon the Lacedaemonians, to get some spoil on a sudden, or to destroy a part of their country: Philopoemen then would ever be **the foremost to**

go out, and the hindermost to come in. When he had leisure, he used much hunting in time of peace, all to acquaint his body with toil and [travail], or else he would be digging of his grounds. For he had a fair manor, not passing twenty furlongs out of the city, whither he would walk commonly after dinner or supper: and then when night came that it was bedtime, he would lie upon some ill-favoured mattress, as [did] the meanest labourer he had, and in the morning by break of the day, he went out either with his vine men to labour in his vineyard, or else with his plough men to follow the plough, and sometimes returned again to the city, and followed matters of the commonwealth, with his friends and other officers of the same. Whatsoever he could spare and get in the wars, he spent it in buying of goodly horses, in making of fair armours, or paying his poor countrymen's ransom, that were taken prisoners in the wars: but for his goods and revenue, he sought only to increase them, by the profit of **tillage**, which he esteemed the justest and best way of getting of goods. For he did not trifle therein, but employed his whole care and study upon it, as one that thought it fit for every noble man and gentleman so to travail, govern, and increase his own, that he should have no occasion to covet or usurp another man's.

He took no pleasure to hear all kind of matters, nor to read all sorts of books of philosophy: but those only that would teach him most to become virtuous. Neither did he much care to read Homer's works, saving those places only that stirred up men's hearts most unto valiantness. But of all other stories, he specially delighted to read Evangelus' books, which treated of the discipline of wars, how to set battles; and declared the acts and **gests** of Alexander the Great, saying: that men should ever bring his words unto deed, unless men would take them for vain stories, and things spoken, but not to profit by. For in his books of the feats of war, and how battles should be ordered, he was not only contented to see them drawn and set out, in [charts] and maps: but would also put them in execution, in the places themselves as they were set out. And therefore, when the army marched in order of battle in the field, he would consider and study with himself, the sudden events and approaches of the enemies, that might light upon them, when they coming down to the valley, or going out of a plain, were to pass a river or a ditch, or through some strait: also when he should spread out his army, or else gather it narrow: and this he did not only forecast by himself, but would also argue the same with the captains that were about him.

For Philopoemen doubtless was one of the odd men of the world, that most esteemed the discipline of war, (and sometime **peradventure** more than he needed) as the most large field and most fruitful ground that valiantness could be exercised in: so that he despised and condemned all that were not soldiers, as men good for nothing.

Narration and Discussion

(You might choose one question to do as a writing assignment.)

Explain Plutarch's comparison of Philopoemen with Epaminondas. What does he mean by "Wherefore it seemeth, that he was a better captain for wars, than a wise governor for peace?"

What was Philopoemen's objection to paying much attention to athletics? Do you think this was a wise decision?

Is it better to have very set routines in our lives, or to be flexible about things (for instance, not fussing if we occasionally miss a meal)? Would one way or the other help you survive better in a crisis?

"For he did not trifle therein, but employed his whole care and study upon it, as one that thought it fit for every noble man and gentleman so to travail, govern, and increase his own, that he should have no occasion to covet or usurp another man's." Philopoemen wanted to be a soldier most of all; so why did he take his farming so seriously?

Lesson Three

Introduction

The year was 222 B.C., and Philopoemen was about 30 years old. He joined with the Macedonians (King Antigonus III, also called Antigonus Doson) to oust the king of Sparta (Cleomenes III) from Megalopolis. Although Antigonus was a bit annoyed that

Philopoemen

Philopoemen took control and led a charge without being so ordered, he had to admit that Philopoemen "did like an experienced commander" (Dryden's translation).

Note: Cleomenes III reigned from 235–222 BC, when Sparta was defeated in this battle. His life will be studied in Plutarch's *Agis and Cleomenes*.

Vocabulary

Lacedaemon: Sparta

made Cleomenes still wait upon him: Dryden translates it "amused Cleomenes," meaning he kept him occupied while the others escaped

Cleomenes' device: his true intention, plan

a great spoil: a great deal of treasure

hard by him: close to him

quagmires: swamps

a dart, having a leather thong on the midst of it: a javelin. There is a 19th-century sculpture you might want to look at online, of Philopoemen pulling out the javelin (Warning: he is not wearing much clothing).

it spited him to the guts: Dryden translates this as "he was transported with the desire of partaking in it." This is a perfect example of North's strong and earthy English vs. Dryden's more academic style.

Reading

When he [Philopoemen] was come now to thirty years of age, Cleomenes, king of **Lacedaemon**, came one night upon the sudden, and gave an assault to the city and got into the marketplace, and won it. Philopoemen hearing of it, ran immediately to the rescue. Nevertheless, though he fought very valiantly, and did like a noble soldier, yet he could not repulse the enemies, nor drive them out of the city. But by this means he got his citizens leisure, and some time to get them out of the town to save themselves, staying those that followed them: and **made Cleomenes still wait upon him**, so that in the end he had much ado to save himself being the last man, and very sore hurt, and his horse also slain under him.

Shortly after, Cleomenes being advertised that the Megalopolitans were gotten into the city of Messina, sent unto them to let them understand, that he was ready to deliver them their city, lands, and goods again. But Philopoemen seeing his countrymen very glad of these news, and that every man prepared to return again in haste: he stayed them with these persuasions, shewing them that **Cleomenes' device** was not to redeliver them their city, but rather to take them together with their city: foreseeing well enough, that he could not continue long there, to keep naked walls and empty houses, and that himself in the end should be compelled to go his way. This persuasion stayed the Megalopolitans, but withal it gave Cleomenes occasion to burn and pluck down a great part of the city, and to carry away a great sum of money, and **a great spoil**.

Afterwards, when King Antigonus was come to aid the Achaians against Cleomenes, and that Cleomenes kept on the top of the mountains of Sellasia, and kept all the passages and ways unto them out of all those quarters: King Antigonus set his army in battle **hard by him**, determining to set upon him, and to drive him thence if he could possibly.

Philopoemen was at that time amongst the horsemen with his citizens, who had the Illyrians on the side of them, being a great number of footmen and excellent good soldiers, which did shut in the tail of all the army. So they were commanded to stand still, and to keep their place, until such time as they shew them a red coat of arms on the top of a pike, from the other wing of the battle, where the king himself stood in person. Notwithstanding this straight commandment, the captains of the Illyrians would abide no longer, but went to see if they could force the Lacedaemonians that kept on the top of the mountains. The Achaians contrariwise, kept their place and order, as they were commanded. Euclidas, Cleomenes' brother, perceiving thus their enemies' footmen were severed from their horsemen, suddenly sent the lightest-armed soldiers and lustiest fellows he had in his bands, to give a charge upon the Illyrians behind, to prove if they could make them turn their faces on them, because they had no horsemen for their guard. This was done, and these light-armed men did marvellously trouble and disorder the

Philopoemen

Illyrians. Philopoemen perceiving that, and considering how these light-armed men would be easily broken and driven back, since occasion [it]self enforced them to it: he went to tell the king's captains of it, that led his men of arms. But when he saw he could not make them understand it, and that they made no reckoning of his reasons, but took him of no skill, because he had not yet attained any credit or estimation to be judged a man that could invent or execute any stratagem of war: he went thither himself, and took his citizens with him.

And at his first coming, he so troubled these light armed-men, that he made them fly, and slew a number of them. Moreover, to encourage the better King Antigonus' men, and to make them give a lusty charge upon the enemies, whilst they were thus troubled and out of order: he left his horse, and marched afoot up hill and down hill, in rough and stony ways, full of springs and **quagmires**, being heavily armed at all pieces as a man at arms, and fighting in this sort very painfully and uneasily, he had both his thighs passed through with **a dart, having a leather thong on the midst of it**. And though the blow did not take much hold of the flesh, yet was it a strong blow, for it pierced both thighs through and through, that the iron was seen on the other side. Then was he so [en]cumbered with this blow, as if he had been shackled with irons on his feet, and knew not what to do: for the leather fastened in the midst of the dart, did grieve him marvellously, when they thought to have pulled the dart out of the place where it entered in, so as never a man about him durst set his hands to it.

Philopoemen on the other side, seeing the fight terrible on either side, and would soon be ended: **it spited him to the guts**, he would so fain have been among them. So at the length he made such struggling, putting back one thigh, and setting forward another, that he [broke the shaft in two], and made them pull out the two truncheons, the one on this side, and the other on the other side. Then when he saw he was at liberty again, he took his sword in his hand, and ran through the midst of them that fought, unto the foremost ranks, to meet with the enemy: so that he gave his men a new courage, and did set them on fire with envy, to follow his valiantness.

After the battle was won, Antigonus asked the Macedonian captains, to prove them: who moved the horsemen to divide themselves, and give the charge, before the sign that was commanded. They answered him, that they were forced to do it against their wills, because a young Megalopolitan gentleman gave a charge with his company, before the sign was given. Then Antigonus laughing, told them: the young gentleman played the part of a wise and valiant captain.

Narration and Discussion

How did Philopoemen convince the people that accepting Cleomenes' offer wasn't a good idea? Have you ever been told (unfairly) to keep quiet because you weren't qualified to offer an opinion on something? Do you think Philopoemen should have been listened to anyway?

How did Philopoemen show bravery and understanding beyond his age and experience?

Lesson Four

Introduction

Philopoemen passed on his skills, discipline and passion to the Achaian cavalry—most of whom had never even bothered to show up for battles before.

Vocabulary

great entertainment: Dryden translates this "very advantageous conditions."

only to continue himself in exercise thereof: to keep himself in practice

muster them: gather them together

by and by upon it: immediately (an earlier use of "by and by")

Reading

This exploit, together with Antigonus' testimony, gave great reputation unto Philopoemen, as we may easily imagine. So King Antigonus marvellously entreated him he would serve with him, and offered him a band of men at arms, and **great entertainment**, if he would go with him. But Philopoemen refused his offer, and chiefly, because he knew his own nature, that he could hardly abide to be commanded by any. Notwithstanding, because he could not be idle, he took sea, and went into Crete, where he knew there were wars, **only to continue himself in exercise thereof**. So when he had served a long time with the Cretans, which were valiant soldiers, and very expert in all policies and feats of war, and moreover were men of a moderate and spare diet: he returned home again to Achaia, with so great credit and reputation of every one, that he was presently chosen general of all the horsemen. So when he entered into his charge, he found many horsemen very ill horsed, upon such [common horses] as might be gotten cheapest, and how they used not to go themselves in person to the wars, but did send others in their stead: and to be short, how they neither had hearts, nor experience of the wars, and all because the generals and captains of the people of the Achaians that served before him, did take no heed to those matters, as fearing to offend any, because they had the greatest authority in their hands, to punish or reward whom they thought good.

Philopoemen fearing none of all these things, would leave no part of his charge and duty undone, but went himself in person to all the cities, to persuade and encourage the young gentlemen, to be well horsed, and well armed, that they might win honour in the field, be able to defend themselves, and overthrow their enemies. And where persuasion could do no good, there he would set fines upon their heads that so refused, and did use to **muster them** oft, and did acquaint them with tilting, turning, and barriers, and one to fight with another, and at such times and places specially, as he knew there would be multitudes of people to give them the looking on: that in short space he made them very forward, proper, and ready horsemen, whose chiefest property is, to keep their order and ranks in the battle. So as when necessity served for the whole company of horsemen to turn together, half turn, or whole turn, or else every man by himself:

they were so thoroughly trained in it, that all the whole troop set in battle [ar]ray, did seem as it were to be but one body, they removed so together, and withal so easily, and at all times, and so oft, as turn they would on the one side, or on the other.

Now in a great battle the Achaians had with the Ætolians and the Elians, by the river of Larissus: Demophantus, general of the horsemen of the Ætolians, came from his company to fight with Philopoemen, who also made towards him, and gave him first such a blow with his spear, that he strake him stark dead. When Demophantus fell to the ground, his soldiers fled **by and by upon it**. This won Philopoemen great honour, who gave no place to the youngest men in fighting most valiantly with his own hands: nor to the oldest men in wisdom, for the wise leading of his army.

Narration and Discussion

What mistake had the former "generals and captains of the people of the Achaians" made?

Why did Philopoemen find it helpful to train his soldiers "at such times and places specially, as he knew there would be multitudes of people to give them the looking on?" In what other ways did he turn these soldiers into a formidable force?

Discuss this passage: "So as when necessity served for the whole company of horsemen to turn together, half turn, or whole turn, or else every man by himself: they were so thoroughly trained in it, that all the whole troop set in battle [ar]ray, did seem as it were to be but one body, they removed so together, and withal so easily, and at all times, and so oft, as turn they would on the one side, or on the other." Christians are familiar with the imagery of "one body," e.g. 1 Corinthians 12, Romans 12. How might Plutarch's description apply to the "body of believers?"

How did Philopoemen prove that he wasn't just "all talk" in the battle with the Ætolians?

Philopoemen

Lesson Five

Introduction

The improved confidence of the Achaian army spread to the other citizens of Megalopolis. Men brought out the household silver to melt down for weapons, and women searched for needles, thread, and flag patterns.

Who was Aratus?

Aratus of Sicyon lived from 271-213 B.C. He was mentioned in the first lesson: "[Ecdemus and Demophanes]... did help Aratus also to drive the tyrant Niocles, out of Sicyone." Plutarch also wrote a *Life of Aratus*.

Vocabulary

> "where any little thing stoppeth and falleth to the bottom, which the course of the water bringeth down the stream, there the rest that followeth doth use to stay, and go no further": Dryden translates this "where, when a few little particles of matter once stop, others stick to them, and one part strengthening another, the whole becomes firm and solid."
>
> **sticking unto King Ptolomy:** trying to win his favour
>
> **strange governors:** foreign commanders
>
> **targets:** shields
>
> **morryans, morions, or burganettes:** helmets
>
> **of sundry colours:** of various colors

Reading

Indeed the first man that made the people of Achaia grow in power and greatness, was Aratus [see note above]: for before his time Achaia was of small reckoning, because the cities of the same stood divided between themselves, and Aratus was the first man that made them join together, and [e]stablished among them an honest civil government. Whereby it happened, that as we see in brooks and rivers **where any little thing stoppeth and falleth to the bottom, which the course of the water bringeth down the stream, there the rest that followeth doth use to stay, and go no further**: even so in the cities of Greece that were in hard state, and sore weakened, by faction one against another, the Achaians were the first that stayed themselves, and grew in amity one with the other, and afterwards drew on the rest of the cities into league with them, as good neighbours and confederates. Some by helping and delivering them from the oppression of tyrants, and winning other also by their peaceable government and good concord: they had in this wise, to bring all the country of Peloponnesus into one body and league. Nevertheless, while Aratus lived, they depended most upon the strength and power of the Macedonians: first with **sticking unto King Ptolomy**, and then unto Antigonus, and last to Philip, who ruled in manner all the state of Greece.

But when Philopoemen came to govern, and to be the chiefest man, the Achaians being strong enough to resist the strongest, would march then no more under any other body's ensign, nor would suffer any more **strange governors** or captains over them. For Aratus (as it seemed) was somewhat too soft and cold for the wars, and therefore the most things he did, were by gentle entreaties, by intelligences, and by the king's friendships with whom he was great, as we have at large declared in his life. But Philopoemen being a man of execution, hardy and valiant of person, and of very good fortune, in the first battle that he ever made, did marvellously increase the courage and hearts of the Achaians: because under his charge they ever foiled their enemies, and always had the upper hand over them.

The first thing Philopoemen began withal at his coming, he changed the manner of setting of their tables, and their fashion of arming themselves. For before they carried little light **targets**, which because they were thin and narrow, did not cover half their bodies, and used spears far shorter than pikes, by reason whereof they were very light, and good to skirmish and fight afar off: but when they came to battle, their enemies then had great [ad]vantage of them. As for the order of their battles, they knew not what it meant, nor to cast themselves into a snail or ring, but only used the square battle

Philopoemen

[formation], nor yet gave it any such front where the pikes of many ranks might push together, and where the soldiers might stand so close, that their targets should touch one another, as they do in the squadron of the battle of the Macedonians: by reason whereof, they were soon broken, and overthrown. Philopoemen reformed all this, persuading them to use the pike and shield, instead of their little [target and spear], and to put good **morryans (morions) or burganettes** on their heads, corselettes on their bodies, and good tasses and greaves to cover their thighs and legs, that they might fight it out manfully, not giving a foot of ground, as light armed men that run to and fro in a skirmish. And thus having persuaded and taught the young men to arm themselves thoroughly, first he made them the bolder and more courageous to fight, as if they had been men that could not have been overcome: then he turned all their vain superfluous charge, into necessary and honest expenses. But he could not possibly bring them altogether from their vain and rich apparel, they had of long time taken up, the one to exceed another: nor from their sumptuous furniture of houses, as in beds, hangings, curious service at the table, and delicate kind[s] of dishes. But to begin to withdraw this desire in them which they had, to be fine and delicate, in all superfluous and unnecessary things, and to like of things necessary, and profitable: he wished them to look more nearly to their ordinary charge about themselves, taking order as well for their apparel, as also for their diet, and to spare in them, to come honourably armed to the field, for defence of their country.

Thereupon, if you had looked into the goldsmiths' shops, you should have seen nothing else in their hands, but breaking and battering of pots of gold and silver, to be cast and molten down again, and then gilding of armours and targets, and silvering of bits. In the showplaces for the running of horses, there was managing and breaking of young horses, and young men exercising arms. Women's hands also were full of **morions** and headpieces, whereto they tied goodly brave plumes of feathers **of sundry colours**, and were also full of embroidered arming coats and cassocks, with curious and very rich works. The sight of which bravery did heave up their hearts, and made them gallant and lively: so as envy bred straight in them who should do best service, and no way spare for the wars. Indeed, sumptuousness and bravery in other sights, doth secretly carry men's minds away, and allure them to seek after vanities, which makes them tender bodied, and womanish persons: because this sweet tickling, and enticing of the outward sense that is delighted therewith, doth straight melt and soften the strength and courage of the mind.

But again, the sumptuous cost bestowed upon warlike furniture, doth encourage and make great a noble heart. Even as Homer sayeth it did Achilles, when Thetis brought him new armour and weapons she had caused Vulcan to make for him, and laid them at his feet: who seeing them, could not tarry, but was straight set on fire with desire to occupy them. So when Philopoemen had brought the youth of Achaia to this good pass, to come thus bravely armed and furnished into the field, he began then to exercise them continually in arms: wherein they did not only shew themselves obedient to him, but did moreover strive one to excel another, and to do better than their fellows. For they liked marvellous well the ordering of the battle he had taught them, because that standing so close together as they did, they thought surely they could hardly be overthrown. Thus by continuance of time, being much used to wear their armour, they found them a great deal easier and lighter than before, besides the pleasure they took to see their armour so brave and so rich: insomuch as they longed for some occasion to try them straight upon their enemies.

Narration and Discussion

Why did the Achaians rely less on foreign support after Philopoemen came to command?

How did Philopoemen "divert the passion" of the officers into more useful channels? How might an employer or a teacher use this strategy?

"But again, the sumptuous cost bestowed upon warlike furniture, doth encourage and make great a noble heart," or as Dryden translates it, "Magnificence of this kind strengthens and heightens the courage." Think of Bilbo Baggins' courage as he held his dagger, or the importance of weapons in the Narnia stories. Think of Excalibur! Why does putting on a new uniform and picking up a decent weapon strengthen one's courage (or does it?)? (You might find the Armour of God/Sword of the Spirit passage useful as you think about this.)

Lesson Six

Introduction

Philopoemen's career was at a high point. Patriotic spirit was running feverishly, and everyone was confident that the Achaian army would win at whatever they did.

Note on the "Statue of Philopoemen at Delphi"

It appears that only the base of the statue still exists. Most of the pictures of the "statue of Philopoemen" are the sculpture of him pulling the javelin out of his leg, not the one referred to here.

Vocabulary

> **They both had entertained in pay a great number of strangers to serve them:** They had both hired a great number of foreign soldiers (mercenaries)
>
> **he was very busy, and earnest still, to follow the chase of them that first fled, and so came hard by the Achaians that stood still in their battle, and kept their ranks:** Machanidas and his mercenaries chased those on the Achaian side who had run away, while the rest of the Achaian army remained in formation (wondering what to do next)
>
> **suffered them to take their course:** let them chase after the fleeing spearmen and Tarentines
>
> **they did not look to fight:** they did not expect to have to fight at all
>
> **he slew him in the ditch:** when Philopoemen stabbed Machanidas, he fell off his horse and into the ditch
>
> **his army ranging in order of battle:** his army showing their maneuvers

Reading

Now the Achaians at that time were at wars with Machanidas, the tyrant of Lacedaemon, who sought by all device he could with a great army, to become chief lord of all the Peloponnesians. When news was brought that Machanidas was come into the country of the Mantineans, Philopoemen straight marched towards him with his army: so they met both not far from the city of Mantinea, where by and by they put themselves in order of battle. **They both had entertained in pay a great number of strangers to serve them**, besides the whole force of their country: and when they came to join battle, Machanidas with his strangers gave such a lusty charge upon certain [spearmen and Tarentines] whom Philopoemen had [placed in the front] to begin the skirmish, that he overthrew them, and made them flee withal.

But where he should have gone on directly against the Achaians that were ranged in battle [ar]ray, to have proved if he could have broken them: **he was very busy, and earnest still, to follow the chase of them that first fled, and so came hard by the Achaians that stood still in their battle, and kept their ranks**. This great overthrow fortuning at the beginning, many men thought the Achaians were but cast away. But Philopoemen made as though it had been nothing, and that he set light by it, and spying the great fault his enemies made, following the forlorn hope on the spur, whom they had overthrown, and straying so far from the battle of their footmen, whom they had left naked, and the field open upon them: he did not make towards them to stay them, nor did strive to stop them that they should not follow those that fled, but **suffered them to take their course**.

And when he saw that they were gone a good way from their footmen, he made his men march upon the Lacedaemonians, whose sides were naked, having no horsemen to guard them: and so did set upon them on the one side, and ran so hastily on them to win one of their flanks, that he made them fly, and slew withal a great number of them. For it is said, there were four thousand Lacedaemonians slain in the field, because they had no man to lead them: and moreover, they say **they did not look to fight**, but supposed rather they had won the field, when they saw Machanidas chasing stil those upon the spur, whom he had overthrown.

Philopoemen

After this, Philopoemen retired to meet Machanidas, who came back from the chase with his strangers. But by chance there was a great broad ditch between them, so as both of them rode upon the banksides of the same, a great while together, one against another of them: the one side seeking some convenient place to get over and fly, and the other side seeking means to keep them from starting away. So, to see the one before the other in this sort, it appeared as they had been wild beasts brought to an extremity, to defend themselves by force, from so fierce a hunter as Philopoemen was. But whilst they were striving thus, the tyrant's horse that was lusty and courageous, and felt the force of his master's spurs pricking in his sides, that the blood followed after, did venture to leap the ditch, coming to the bank side, stood upon his hindmost legs, and advanced forward with his foremost feet, to reach to the other side.

Then Simmias and Polyaenus, who were about Philopoemen when he fought, ran thither straight to keep him [Machanidas] in with their staves that he should not leap the ditch. But Philopoemen who was there before them, perceiving that the tyrant's horse by lifting up his head so high, did cover all his master's body: forsook by and by his horse, and took his spear in both his hands, and thrust at the tyrant with so good a will, that **he slew him in the ditch**. In memory whereof, the Achaians that did highly esteem this valiant act of his, and his wisdom also in leading of the battle: did set up his image in brass, in the temple of Apollo in Delphi, in the form he slew the tyrant.

They say, that at the assembly of the common games called Nemea, (which they solemnise in honour of Hercules, not far from the city of Argos) and not long after he had won this battle of Mantinea, [having been] made general the second time of the tribe of the Achaians, and being at good leisure also by reason of the feast: he first shewed all the Grecians that were come thither to see the games and pastimes, **his army ranging in order of battle**, and made them see how easily they removed their places every way, as necessity and occasion of fight required, without troubling or confounding their ranks, and that with a marvellous force and readiness.

When he had done this, he went into the Theater to hear the musicians play, and sing to their instruments, who should win the best game, being accompanied with lusty young gentlemen appareled in purple cloaks, and in scarlet coats and cassocks they wore upon their armour, being all in the flower of their youth, and well given and disposed: who did greatly honour and reverence their captain, and besides that, shewed themselves inwardly of noble hearts, being encouraged by many notable battles they had fought, in which they had ever attained the victory, and gotten the upper hand of their enemies. And by chance, as they were entered into the Theater, Pylades the musician, singing certain poems of Timotheus, called the Perses, fell into these verses:

> O Greeks it is even he, which your prosperity
> Hath given to you: and therewithal! a noble liberty.
>
> [Dryden: "Under his conduct Greece was glorious and was free."]

When he had sweetly song out aloud these noble verses, passingly well made: the whole assembly of the Grecians in the Theater, that were gathered thither to see the games, cast all their eyes straight upon Philopoemen, and clapped their hands one to another for joy, because of the great hope they had in him, that through him they should soon recover their ancient reputation, and so imagined they possessed already the noble and worthy minds of their ancestors.

Narration and Discussion

"[They] cast all their eyes straight upon Philopoemen, and clapped their hands one to another for joy..." How did Philopoemen's life so far prepare him for this moment of applause? Do you feel it was deserved?

Note this phrase: "and so imagined they possessed already the noble and worthy minds of their ancestors." The Achaians applauded Philopoemen, but they took the credit somewhat for themselves, like fans cheering for a winning sports team. Was this a good thing?

Lesson Seven

Introduction

Plutarch gives examples of how Philopoemen was respected and feared: his name alone was enough to give his enemies nightmares. Even when he was officially out of command for awhile, he was still The Commander. But at the same time, it's acknowledged (for the first time) that Philopoemen had "ill-wishers"—and at one point he was even threatened with banishment.

This passage moves around in time, and several separate incidents are described. I have divided the text into three sections, which could be read and narrated separately.

Vocabulary

> **their ordinary riders:** their usual riders
>
> **because they were afraid to hear his name only, as it seemed by their doings:** Dryden translates this "but, as appeared in several occasions, were frighted with his very name." Their actions proved that they were afraid of Philopoemen.
>
> **Nabis:** the tyrant (ruler) of Lacedaemon (Sparta) at that time.
>
> **Philopoemen being then a private man, and having no charge of soldiers:** Philopoemen was temporarily out of command
>
> **Lysippus:** the general of the Achaians while Philopoemen was out of office
>
> **not staying for the assembly of the Megalopolitans**: not waiting for them
>
> **durst not tarry him:** dared not stay there. Dryden says, "thought it not convenient to stay."
>
> **dispraised**: criticized, reproached
>
> **hard at:** right at, on top of
>
> **perceiving his countrymen made no more account of him**: seeing he was out of favour
>
> **diverse**: in this context, it means "various" or "several"

Reading

Part One

And as young horse[s] that do always look to be ridden by **their ordinary riders**, if any stranger get up on their backs, do straight wax strange to be handled, and make great ado: even so, when the Achaians came to any dangerous battle, their hearts were even done, if they had any other general or leader than Philopoemen, on whom still they depended and looked. And when they saw him ever, the whole army rejoiced, and desired straight to be at it, they had such confidence in his valiantness and good fortune: and truly not without cause. For of all men, their enemies did fear him most, and durst not stand before him: **because they were afraid to hear his name only, as it seemed by their doings**.

For Philip king of Macedon, imagining that if he could find means to dispatch Philopoemen out of the way, howsoever it were, the Achaians would straight take part again with him: [he] sent men secretly into the city of Argos, to kill him by treason. Howbeit the practise was discovered, and the king [Philip] ever after was mortally hated of all the Grecians generally, and taken for a cowardly and wicked Prince.

Part Two

It fortuned one day when the Boeotians laid siege to the city of Megara, and thought certainly to have won it at the first assault: there rose a rumour suddenly amongst them, that Philopoemen came to aid the city, and was not far from it only with his army. But it was a false report. Notwithstanding, the Boeotians were so scared, that for fear they left scaling ladders behind them, which they had set against the walls to have scaled the town, and fled straight to save themselves.

Part Three

Another time, when **Nabis** the tyrant of Lacedaemon, that succeeded Machanidas, had taken the city of Messina upon the sudden:

Philopoemen

Philopoemen being then a private man, and having no charge of soldiers, [Philopoemen] went unto **Lysippus**, general of the Achaians that year, to persuade him that he would send present aid unto them of Messina. Lysippus told him, it was to late now to go thither, and that it was but a lost town, not to be helped: considering the enemies were in it already. Philopoemen perceiving he could not procure him to go, went thither himself with the force of Messina only, **not staying for the assembly of the Megalopolitans**, that were in counsel about it, to give him commission by voices of the people to take them with him: but they all willingly followed him, as if he had been their continual general, and the man that by nature was worthiest of all other to command them.

Now when he came near unto Messina, Nabis hearing of his coming, **durst not tarry him**, though he had his army within the city, but stole out at another gate [with his men], and marched away in all the haste he could, thinking himself a happy man [if] he could so escape his hands, and retire with safety, as indeed he did. And thus was Messina, by [Philopoemen's] means, delivered from captivity.

All that we have written hitherto concerning Philopoemen, falleth out doubtless to his great honour and glory: but afterwards he was greatly **dispraised** for a journey he made into Crete, at the request of the Gortynians, who sent to pray him to be their captain, being sore troubled with wars at that time. Because Philopoemen went then to serve the Gortynians, when the tyrant Nabis had greatest wars with the Megalopolitans, in their own country: they laid it to his charge, either that he did it to flee the wars, or else that he sought honour out of season with foreign nations, when his poor citizens the Megalopolitans were in such distress, that their country being lost and destroyed, they were driven to keep them within their city, and to sow all their [streets] with corn, to sustain them withal, when their enemies were encamped almost hard at their town gates.

And the rather, because himself making wars with the Cretans, and serving strangers beyond the sea in the meantime, gave his enemies occasion to slander him that he fled, that he would not tarry to fight for defence of his country. Again, there were that, because the Achaians did choose other for their general, that he being a private man and without charge, was the rather contented to be general of the Gortynians, who had marvellously entreated him to take the charge: for he was a man that could not abide to live idly, and that desired specially above all things to serve continually in the wars, and to put in practise his skill and discipline in the leading of an army.

The words he spake one day of king Ptolomy doth witness as much. For when there were some that praised king Ptolomy highly, saying that he trained his army well, and that he still continued his person in exercise of arms: [Philopoemen said,] It is not commendable for a king of his years, to delight in training his men to exercise arms, but to do some act himself in person. [*Dryden's version: "And what praise," replied Philopoemen, "for a king of his years, to be always preparing, and never performing?"*]

Well, in the end, the Megalopolitans took his absence in such evil part, that they thought it a piece of treason, and would needs have banished him, and put him from the freedom of the city: had not the Achaians sent their general Aristaenetus unto them, who would not suffer the sentence of banishment to pass against him, although otherwise there was ever contention between them about matters of the commonwealth. Afterwards, Philopoemen **perceiving his countrymen made no more account of him**, to spite them withal, he made **diverse** small villages and cities rebel against them, and taught them to say, and to give it out, that they were not their subjects, neither paid them tribute from the beginning: and he made them stand to it openly, and maintain their sedition against the city of Megalopolis, before the council of the Achaians. These things happened shortly after.

Narration and Discussion

Why would Philopoemen go to the Gortynians, when his own country needed him?

Discuss the idea that well-trained horses may only be managed by their usual trainers or riders. Does that make them too dependent? What would happen if their leader was injured or killed? (Consider the earlier statement that soldiers should be trained for flexibility, unlike athletes who can perform only under certain conditions.)

Comment on Philopoemen's opinion of Ptolomy [Ptolemy]—"always preparing and never performing."

Philopoemen

Explain how Philopoemen found himself out of favour, and how he reacted. Do you feel his attempts at retribution were justified?

Lesson Eight

Introduction

This lesson opens with Philopoemen still in Crete, which added to his reputation as a general. From here on the story is a string of good things, bad things. A bad thing: Philopoemen returned home to Megalopolis, and found things in chaos. A worse thing: he took his men to sea to fight Nabis of Sparta, and nearly sank the ship. Good thing: it didn't sink, and he ended up winning a battle on land. Bad thing: Nabis surprised them. Good thing: Philopoemen chased Nabis's army away, and caught many Spartans sneaking back later on.

Vocabulary

he shewed not himself a Peloponnesian, nor like a man born in Arcadia: he didn't act like this, although he was one

Philip: the king of Macedon (the territory north of Greece)

Titus Quintius Flamininus: a Roman consul at this time. Plutarch uses his *Life* as a parallel to that of Philopoemen.

fine devices: crafty tricks

would needs take upon him to do the same: insisted on doing the same

diverse: multiple

ere they wist it: before they knew anything about it

in this fear and hurly burly: commotion, tumult

through a marvellous ill and dangerous way: through rough country

made the Achaians amazed: dismayed them

wherein he was compassed: in the place where he was surrounded

Reading

But whilst [Philopoemen] made wars in Crete for the Gortynians, **he shewed not himself a Peloponnesian, nor like a man born in Arcadia**, to make plain and open wars: but he had learned the manner of the Cretans, to use their own policies, **fine devices**, and ambushes against themselves, made them know also, that all their crafts, were but childish sports as it were: in respect of those that were devised, and put in execution, by a wise experienced captain, and skillful to fight a battle.

So, Philopoemen having won great fame by his acts done in Crete, returned again to Peloponnesus, where he found, that **Philip** king of Macedon had been overcome in battle, by **Titus Quintius Flamininus**: and that the Achaians joining with the Romans, did make war against the tyrant Nabis, against whom he was made general immediately upon his return, and gave battle by sea. In the which it seemed he fell into like misfortune, as Epaminondas did: the event of this battle falling out much worse with him, than was looked for, in respect of his former courage and valiantness. But as for Epaminondas, some say he returned willingly out of [Asia and the Islands], without any exploit done, because he would not have his countrymen fleshed with spoil by sea, as fearing least of valiant soldiers by land, they would by little and little (as Plato) become dissolute mariners by sea.

But Philopoemen contrariwise, presuming upon the skill he had to set the battle in good order by land, **would needs take upon him to do the same** by sea. But he was taught to his cost to know what exercise and experience meant, and how strong it maketh them that are practised in things. For he lost not only the battle by sea, being unskillful of that service: but he committed besides a fouler error. For that he caused an old ship to be rigged, which had been very good of service before, but not occupied in forty years together, and embarked his countrymen into the same, which were all likely to perish, because the ship had **diverse** leaks.

This overthrow made his enemies despise him utterly, who persuaded themselves he was fled for altogether, and had given them sea room: whereupon [in contempt of him] they laid siege to the city of Gythium. Philopoemen being advertised thereof, embarked his men suddenly, and set upon his enemies **ere they wist it**, or had any thought of his coming: and found them straggling up and down, without watch or guard, by reason of the victory they had lately won. So he landed his men closely by night, and went and set fire upon his enemies' camp, and burnt it every whit: and **in this fear and hurly burly**, slew a great number of them.

Shortly after this stealing upon them, the tyrant Nabis also stole upon him again unawares, as he was to go **through a marvellous ill and dangerous way**. Which **made the Achaians amazed** at the first, thinking it unpossible for them that they could ever [e]scape that danger, considering their enemies kept all the ways thereabouts. But Philopoemen bethinking himself, and considering the nature and situation of the place: after he had viewed it well, he shewed them plainly then, that the chiefest point of a good soldier, and man of war, was to know how to put an army in battle, according to the time and situation of the place. For he did but alter the form of his battle a little, and sorted it according to the situation of the place, **wherein he was compassed**: and by doing this without trouble or business, he took away all fear of danger, and gave a charge upon his enemies in such fierce wise, that in a short time he put them all to flight. [*Dryden: For by advancing only a few paces, and, without any confusion or trouble, altering his order according to the nature of the place, he immediately relieved himself from every difficulty, and then charging, put the enemy to flight.*]

And when he perceived that they did not flee all in troops together towards the city, but scattering wise, abroad in the fields in every place: he caused the trumpet to sound the retreat. Then he commanded the chase to be followed no further, for that all the country thereabout was full of thick woods and groves, very ill for horsemen: and also because there were many brooks, valleys, and quagmires which they should pass over, he encamped himself presently, being yet broad day. And so, fearing least his enemies would in the night time draw unto the city, one after another, and by couples: he sent a great number of Achaians, and laid them in ambush amongst the brooks and hills near about it, which made great slaughter of Nabis' soldiers, because they came not altogether in troops, but scatteringly one after another as they fled, one here, another there, and so fell into their enemies' hands, as birds into the fowler's net.

Discussion and Narration

"Altering his order according to the nature of the place." Was it effective for Philopoemen to fight the enemy by making use of their own strategies, rather than insisting on fighting like a Peloponnesian?

"But he was taught to his cost to know what exercise and experience meant, and how strong it maketh them that are practised in things." Why was Philopoemen's great experience in land fighting not enough to prepare him for a sea battle? What other problems did he have?

Lesson Nine

Introduction

In this passage we hear of more secret ill-will, and jealousy of Philopoemen by the Roman consul Titus Flamininus (because Philopoemen was just a common Arcadian). However, he did gain almost everyone's respect at this time by persuading the Spartans to join the Achaian League (198 B.C.).

Vocabulary

> **a mean gentleman of Arcadia:** a common or lowly Arcadian.
>
> **their tribe and communality:** their confederacy, union
>
> **they might command their virtue upon any occasion, without cost unto them:** they could have their goodwill without bribes, for free

Reading

These acts made Philopoemen singularly beloved of the Grecians, and they did him great honour in all their Theaters and common assemblies. Whereat Titus Quintius Flamininus, of nature very ambitious, and covetous of honour: did much repine, and was envious at the matter, thinking that a Consul of Rome should have place and honour amongst the Achaians, before **a mean gentleman**

of Arcadia. And he imagined he had deserved better of all Greece, than Philopoemen had: considering, how by the only proclamation of an herald, he had restored Greece again to her ancient liberty, which before his coming was subject unto King Philip, and unto the Macedonians.

Afterwards, Titus Quintius made peace with the tyrant Nabis. Nabis was shortly after very traitorously slain by the Ætolians. Whereupon the city of Sparta grew to a tumult, and Philopoemen straight taking the occasion, went thither with his army, and handled the matter so wisely: that partly for love, and partly by force, he won the city, and joined it unto the tribe of the Achaians.

So was he marvellously commended and esteemed of the Achaians for this notable victory, to have won **their tribe and communality** so famous a city, and of so great estimation. For the city of Sparta was no small increase of their power. Moreover he won by this means, the love and good will of all the honest men of Lacedaemon, of the hope they had to find him a protector and defender of their liberty.

Wherefore, when the tyrant Nabis' house and goods were sold, as forfeited to the state: they resolved in their council to make him a present of the money thereof, which amounted to the sum of six score talents, and [they] sent ambassadors purposely unto him, to offer it him. Then Philopoemen shewed himself plainly to be no counterfeit honest man, but a good man indeed. For first of all, there was not one of all the Lacedaemonians that durst presume to offer him this money, but every man was afraid to tell him of it: and everybody that was appointed to do it, made some excuse or other for themselves. Notwithstanding, in the end they made one Timolaus to take the matter upon him, who was his familiar friend, and also his host. And yet the same Timolaus when he came unto Megalopolis, and was lodged and entertained in Philopoemen's house, did so much reverence him for his wise talk and conversation, for his moderate diet, and just dealing with all men: that he saw there was no likely possibility to corrupt him with money, so as he durst not once open his mouth to speak to him of the present he had brought him, but found some other occasion to excuse the cause of his coming unto him.

And being sent unto him again the second time, he did even as much as at the first time. And making a third proof, he ventured at the last to open the matter unto him, and told him the good will the city of Sparta did bear him. Philopoemen became a glad man to hear it: and when he had heard all he had to say to him, he went himself unto the city of Sparta. There he declared unto the council, that it was not honest men, and their good friends, they should seek to win and corrupt with money, considering **they might command their virtue upon any occasion, without cost unto them**: but that they should seek to bribe naughty men with money, and such as by seditious orations in council did mutiny, and put a whole city in uproar: to the end that having their mouths stopped with gifts, they should trouble them the less in the commonwealth. For, said he, it is more necessary to stop your enemies' mouths, and to sew up their lips from liberty of speaking: than it is to keep your friends from it. So noble a man was Philopoemen against all covetousness of money.

Narration and Discussion

How did Philopoemen manage to bring Sparta into the Achaian League? And why did he do this?

What was the difficulty in giving Philopoemen a thank-you gift (or a gesture-of-good-will gift) from the Spartans?

What was Philopoemen's advice about gifts/bribes?

What does the Bible say about bribes? (Check the book of Proverbs.)

Lesson Ten

Introduction

We know that Philopoemen was admired for his integrity and for his military leadership. But in this passage, *first*, he showed good judgment and restraint, and managed to handle Sparta during a dispute—even flouting Titus Flamininus. *Second* (later), he treated the Spartans brutally, took many of them to Achaia, ruined their laws and government, and generally tried to break them into submission. They submitted, but turned to Rome for help as soon as they could. *Third*, during Philopoemen's next period out of office, he kept saying what he would do if he was in charge (sounding more than a little like sour grapes). *Fourth*, he went against a motion to send the Spartans home, but didn't carry it out until he was general again—so that he got the credit for a good action.

Vocabulary

puissant: powerful

but then rather to dissemble it, and not to seem to bear any fault whatsoever they did: Dryden translates this "to keep a watchful eye over them, and dissembling, and putting up with any less important grievances." To dissemble is to conceal one's true motives, feelings, or beliefs. Philopoemen didn't want Diophanes to do anything hot-headed that would put Achaia at risk of invasion by the other powers.

seditions: treasonous plots

a goodly fair walk: a colonnade

to put their heads in the collar: to be humble and submissive

in the cellars and tippling houses: in the drinking places

choler: anger

Reading

Part One

Shortly after, the Lacedaemonians beginning to stir again, Diophanes (who was then general of the Achaians) being advertised of it, began to prepare to punish them. The Lacedaemonians on the other side preparing for the wars, did set all the country of Peloponnesus in arms. Hereupon Philopoemen sought to pacify Diophanes' anger, declaring unto him, that King Antiochus, and the Romans, being at wars together at that present time, and they both having **puissant** armies one against another in the midst of Greece: it was meet for a good general and wise governor, to have an eye to their doings, to be careful of the same, and to beware that he did not trouble or alter any thing within his country at that instant, **but then rather to dissemble it, and not to seem to bear any fault whatsoever [the Spartans] did**. Diophanes would not be persuaded, but entered the territories of Lacedaemon with Quintius Flamininus with him: and together marched directly towards the city of Sparta.

Philopoemen was so mad with their doings, that he took upon him an enterprise not very lawful, nor altogether noble; nevertheless, his attempt proceeded of a noble mind, and great courage. For he got into the city of Sparta, and being but a private person, kept out the general of the Achaians, and the Consul of the Romans from entering the city: and when he had pacified all troubles and **seditions** in the same, he delivered it up again as it was before, into the hands of the communality of the Achaians.

Part Two

Nevertheless, himself being afterwards general of the Achaians, [upon some new misdemeanour of the Lacedaemonians, he] did compel the Lacedaemonians to receive those home again whom they had banished for certain faults, and did put fourscore natural born citizens of Sparta unto death, as Polybius writeth. Or three hundred and fifty, as Aristocrates, another historiographer, reciteth.

Then he pulled down the walls of the city, and razed them to the ground, and took away the most part of their territories, and gave them to the Megalopolitans. All those whom the tyrants had made free denizens [citizens] of Sparta, he compelled them to depart the country of Lacedaemon, and forced them to dwell in Achaia, three thousand only excepted, who would not obey his commandment: all those he sold for slaves, and with the money he made of them (to spite them the more) he built **a goodly fair walk** within the city of Megalopolis.

Yet furthermore, to do the Lacedaemonians all the mischief he could, and as it were, to tread them under the feet in their most grievous misery: he did a most cruel and unjust act toward them. For he compelled them to leave the discipline and manner of education of their children, which Lycurgus had of old time instituted: and made them to follow the manner the Achaians used, in lieu of their old grounded custom, because he saw they would never be humble minded, so long as they kept Lycurgus' order and institution. Thus were they driven **to put their heads in the collar**, by the miserable mishap that befell them: and in all despite, to suffer Philopoemen in this manner to cut asunder (as it were) the sinews of their commonwealth.

But afterwards they made suit to the Romans, that they might be suffered to enjoy their ancient discipline [of education] again, which being granted them, they straight left the manner of the Achaians, and did set up again as much as was possible (after so great misery and corruption of their manners) their old ancient customs and orders of their country.

Part Three

Now about the time the wars began in Greece, between the Romans and King Antiochus, Philopoemen was then a private man, and without any authority. He seeing that King Antiochus lay still in the city of Chalcis, and did nothing but feast and love, and had married a young maid far unmeet for his years: and perceiving that his Syrian soldiers wandered up and down the towns in great disorder, playing many lewd parts without guide of captains: he was very sorry he was not at that time general of the Achaians, and told the Romans, that he envied their victory, having wars with enemies that were so easily to be overcome. For [he said] if fortune favoured me that I were general of the Achaians at this present, I would have killed them every man **in the cellars and tippling houses**.

Now when the Romans had overcome Antiochus, they began to have surer footing in Greece: and to compass in the Achaians of all sides, and specially by reason the heads and governors of the cities about them did yield to the Romans, to win their favour. And now their greatness grew in haste, by the favour of the gods, so as they were become the monarch of the whole world, who brought them now to the end that fortune had determined. Philopoemen in the meantime did like a good pilot, bare hard against the billows and roughness of their waves: and though for the time he was forced to give place, and to let things pass, yet for all that he was against the Romans, and did withstand them in the most part of their proceedings, by seeking ever to defend the liberty of those, who by their eloquence and well doing carried great authority among the Achaians. And when Aristaenetus Megalopolitan, (a man of great authority among the Achaians, and one that ever bare great devotion to the Romans) [said] in open Senate among the Achaians, that they should deny the Romans nothing, nor shew themselves unthankful to them: Philopoemen hearing what he [said], held his peace awhile, and suffered him to speak (though it boiled in his heart, he was so angry with him) and in the end, breaking all patience, and as one overcome with **choler**, he [said]: O Aristaenetus, why have you such haste to see the unfortunate end of Greece?

Part Four

Another time, when Manius, consul of Rome (after he had conquered king Antiochus) did make request to the council of the Achaians, that such as were banished from Lacedaemon, might return home into their country again, and that Titus Quintius Flamininus also did earnestly entreat them: Philopoemen was against it, not from any hatred he bare unto the banished men, but because he would have done it by his own mean[s], and the only grace of the Achaians, to the end they should not be behold[en] for so good a turn, neither unto Titus, nor yet to the Romans.

Afterwards he himself, being general of the Achaians, did restore them wholly to their own again. Thus was Philopoemen sometime, a little too bold and quarrellous, by reason of his great stomach: and specially when any man of authority sought for to have things. [*This rather curious sentence is translated by Dryden as "So impatient was his spirit of any subjection and so prone his nature to contest everything with men in power." Not sure where the stomach went.*]

Narration and Discussion

Are there limits even on what a good man can do without being tempted?

Consider the saying "power corrupts." Up until this time, it seems that was exactly what Philopoemen couldn't be—corrupted. He wouldn't take a bribe and never thought much of personal pleasures. But to the Spartans he now showed cruelty and intolerance; when he was out of office, he showed a "bad attitude." He also delayed doing a good action until it was to his own advantage. Is all this inconsistent with what we know of Philopoemen?

Did Philopoemen really put his country first?

Lesson Eleven

Introduction

General Philopoemen, at seventy years old, wanted to end his years quietly, but couldn't seem to retire. When he heard of a chance to defeat an old enemy, he charged ahead—not suspecting that this would be his last battle.

Vocabulary

> **surceased:** ceased
>
> **had withdrawn the city of Messina from the devotion of the Achaians:** had induced Messina to revolt from the Achaians
>
> **ague:** chills (and fever)
>
> **environed:** surrounded
>
> **he had spurred him that he was all of a gore blood:** he had spurred his horse so much that it was bleeding
>
> **that did not let him:** that did not hinder or stop him
>
> **gibbet:** gallows

Reading

Lastly, being three score and ten years of age, he was the eighth time chosen general of the Achaians, and hoped well, not only to pass the year of his charge in peace and quietness, but also all the rest of his life without any stir of new wars, he saw the affairs of Greece take so good success. For like as the force and strength of sickness declineth, as the natural strength of the sickly body impaireth: so through all the cities and people of Greece, envy of quarrel and wars **surceased**, as their power diminished. Nevertheless, in the end of his year's government, the gods divine (who justly punish all insolent words and deeds) threw him to the ground, as they suffer a rider unfortunately to take a fall off his horse, being come almost to the end of his career. For they write, that he being in a place on a time amongst good company, where one was marvellously praised for a good captain, said unto them: Why, masters, can ye commend him that was contented to be taken prisoner alive of his enemies?

Shortly after came news that Dinocrates Messenian (a private enemy of Philopoemen for certain controversies past between them, and a man generally hated besides, of all honourable and virtuous men, for his licentious wicked life) **had withdrawn the city of Messina from the devotion of the Achaians:** and moreover that he came with an army to take a town called Colonide. Philopoemen was at that time in the city of Argos, sick of an **ague**, and yet hearing these news, took his journey toward Megalopolis, making all the haste he could possible, so that he came above four hundred furlongs that day. Straight he departed thence toward Messina, and tarried not, but took with him a company of men at arms of the lustiest and wealthiest Megalopolitans: who were all young noble men of the city, and willingly offered themselves to go with him for the goodwill they bare him, and for the desire they had to follow his valiantness.

Thus went they on their way towards the city of Messina, and marched so long, that they came near unto the hill of Evander, where they met with Dinocrates Mons and his company, and gave so fierce an onset on them, that they made them all turn tail: howbeit in the meanwhile, there came a relief of five hundred men to Dinocrates, which he had left to keep the country of Messina. The flying men that were scattered here and there, seeing this supply, gathered themselves again together, and shewed upon the hills. Philopoemen fearing to be **environed**, and being desirous to bring his men safe home again, who most of love had followed him: began to march away through narrow bushy places, himself being in the rearward, and turned oftentimes upon his enemies, and skirmished with them, only to drive them away from following of the rest of his company, and not a man that durst once set upon him: for they did but cry out aloof, and wheel as it were about him. Howbeit Philopoemen sundry times venturing far from his company, to give these young noble men leisure to save themselves one after another: took no heed to himself that he was alone, **environed** on every side with a great number of enemies. Notwithstanding, of all his enemies there was not a man that durst come to hand strokes with him, but still slinging and shooting at him afar off, they drave him in the end amongst stony places between hewn rocks, where he had much ado to guide his horse, although **he had spurred him that he was all of a gore blood**. And as for his age, **that did not let him** but he might have saved himself, for he was strong and lusty by the continual exercise he took: but by cursed hap, his body being weak with sickness, and weary with the long journey he had made that day, he found himself very heavy and ill disposed, that his horse stumbling with him, threw him to the ground. His fall was very great, and bruised all his head, that he lay for dead in the place a great while, and never stirred nor spake: so that his enemies thinking he had been dead, came to turn his body to strip him. But when they saw him lift up his head and open his eyes, then many of them fell all at once upon him, and took him, and bound both his hands behind him, and did all the villainy and mischief they could unto him, and such, as one would little have thought Dinocrates would have used in that sort, or that he could have had such an ill thought towards him.

So, they that tarried behind in the city of Messina, were marvellous glad when they heard these news, and ran all to the gates of the city to see him brought in. When they saw him thus shamefully bound, and pinioned, against the dignity of so many honours as he had received, and of so many triumphs and victories as he had passed: the most part of them wept for pity, to consider the mishap and ill fortune of man's nature, where there is so little certainty, as in manner it is nothing. Then began there some courteous speech to run in the mouths of the people by little and little, that they should remember the great good he had done unto them in times past, and the liberty he had restored them unto, when he expulsed the tyrant Nabis out of Messina.

But there were other again (howbeit very few) that to please Dinocrates, said they should hang him on a **gibbet**, and put him to death as a dangerous enemy, and that [he] would never forgive [a] man that had once offended him: and the rather, because he would be more terrible to Dinocrates, than ever he was before, if he escaped his hands, receiving such open shame by him. Nevertheless, in the end they carried him into a certain dungeon under the ground, called the treasury, (which had neither light nor air at all into it, nor door, nor half-door, but a great stone rolled on the mouth of the dungeon) and so they did let him down the same, and stopped the hole again with the stone, and watched it with armed men for to keep him.

Now when these young noble Achaian horsemen had fled upon the spur a great way from the enemy, they remembered themselves, and looked round about for Philopoemen: and finding him not in sight, they supposed straight he had been slain. Thereupon they stayed a great while, and called for him by name, and perceiving he answered not, they began to say among themselves, they were beasts and cowards to flee in that sort: and how they were dishonoured for ever to have forsaken their captain, to save themselves, who had not spared his own life, to deliver them from danger. Hereupon riding on their way, and enquiring still for him: they were in the end advertised how he was taken. And then they went and carried those news through all the towns and cities of Achaia, which were very sorry for him, and took it as a sign of great ill fortune toward them. Whereupon they agreed to send ambassadors forthwith to the Messenians, to demand him: and in the meantime every man should prepare to arm themselves, to go thither, and get him either by force or love.

Narration and Discussion

Discuss Philopoemen's comment in the first paragraph. How was it prophetic?

Show how Philopoemen remained a good general to the end.

Lesson Twelve

Introduction

The death of Philopoemen seemed to the Achaians "the loss of their own greatness," in more ways than one.

Who was Lycortas?

Besides being a friend of Philopoemen, he was also the father of the historian Polybius.

Vocabulary

> **When the Achaians had thus sent:** When they made their intentions known
>
> **hangman:** executioner
>
> **make themselves away:** kill themselves
>
> **gibbet:** gallows
>
> **listed:** desired, chose (a **list** is a desire)
>
> **his convoy:** his funeral procession

Reading

When the Achaians had thus sent, Dinocrates feared nothing so much, as that delay of time might save Philopoemen's life: wherefore to prevent it, as soon as night came, and that the people were at rest, he straight caused the stone to be rolled from the mouth of the dungeon, and willed the hangman to be let down to Philopoemen with a cup of poison to offer him, who was commanded also not to go from him, until he had drunk it.

When the **hangman** was come down, he found Philopoemen laid on the ground upon a little cloak, having no **list** to sleep, he was so grievously troubled in his mind. Who when he saw light, and the man standing by him, holding a cup in his hand with this poison, he sat upright upon his couch, howbeit with great pain he was so weak: and taking the cup in his hand, asked the hangman if he heard any news of the horsemen that came with him, and specially of Lycortas. The hangman made him answer, that the most of them were saved. Then he [Philopoemen] cast his hands a little over his head, and looking merely on him he [said]: It is well, seeing we are not all unfortunate.

Therewith speaking no more words, nor making other ado, he drank up all the poison, and laid him down as before. So nature strave not much withal, his body being brought so low, and thereupon the poison wrought his effect, and rid him straight out of his pain.

The news of his death ran presently through all Achaia, which generally from high to low was lamented. Whereupon all the Achaian youth and councillors of their cities and towns, assembled themselves in the city of Megalopolis, where they all agreed without delay to revenge his death. They made Lycortas their General, under whose conduct they invaded the Messenians, with force and violence, putting all to the fire and sword: so as the Messenians were so feared with this merciless fury, that they yielded themselves, and wholly consented to receive the Achaians into their city. But Dinocrates would not give them leisure to execute him by justice, for he killed himself: and so did all the rest **make themselves away**, who gave advice that Philopoemen should be put to death. But those that would have had Philopoemen hanged on a **gibbet**, Lycortas caused them to be taken, which afterwards were put to death with all kind of torments. That done, they burnt Philopoemen's body, and did put his ashes into a pot.

Then they [the Achaians] straight departed from Messina, not in disorder, one upon another's neck as every man **listed**: but in such an order and [ar]ray, that in the midst of these funerals they did make a triumph of victory. For the soldiers were all crowned with garlands of laurel in token of victory; notwithstanding, the tears ran down their cheeks in token of sorrow, and they led their enemies prisoners, shackled and chained. The funeral pot in the which were Philopoemen's ashes, was so covered with garlands of flowers, nosegays, and laces, that it could scant be seen or discerned, and was carried by one Polybius a young man, the son of Lycortas, that was general at that time to the Achaians: about whom there marched all the noblest and chiefest of the Achaians, and after them also followed all the soldiers armed, and their horses very well furnished. The rest, they were not so sorrowful in their countenance, as they are commonly which have great cause of sorrow: nor yet so joyful, as those that came conquerors from so great a victory. Those of the cities, towns, and villages in their way as they passsed, came and presented themselves unto them, to touch the funeral pot of his ashes, even as they were wont to take him by the hand, and to make much of him when he was returned from the wars: and did accompany **his convoy** unto the city of Megalopolis. At the gates whereof, were old men, women, and children, which thrusting themselves amongst the soldiers, did renew the tears, sorrows, and lamentations of all the miserable and unfortunate city: who took it that they had lost with their citizen, the first and chiefest place of honour among the Achaians. So he was buried very honourably as appertained unto him: and the other prisoners of Messina, were all stoned to death, about his sepulchre. All the other cities of Achaia, besides many other honours they did unto him, did set up statues, and as like to him, as could be counterfeited.

Afterwards in the unfortunate time of Greece, when the city of Corinth was burnt and destroyed by the Romans, there was a malicious Roman that did what he could to have the same pulled down again, by burdening and accusing Philopoemen (as if he had been alive) that he was always enemy to the Romans, and envied much their prosperity and victories. But after Polybius had answered him: neither the Consul Mummius, nor his counsellors, nor lieutenants, would suffer them to deface and take away the honours done in memory of so famous and worthy a man, although he had many ways done much hurt unto Titus Quintius Flamininus, and unto Manius. So, these good men then made a difference between duty and profit: and did think honesty and profit two distinct things, and so separated one from the other, according to reason and justice. Moreover they were persuaded, that like as men receive courtesy and goodnes of any, so are they bound to requite them again, with kindness and duty. And as men use to acknowledge the same: even so ought men to honour and reverence virtue. And thus much for the life of Philopoemen.

Narration and Discussion

Discuss Philopoemen's last words. How was his attitude at the end consistent with the rest of his life?

How did the people of Megalopolis react to his death? How did Philopoemen's death symbolize the end of an era?

For further study:

The writings of Polybius about this time are very interesting and add a different perspective to what Plutarch has to say (he explains more about the Roman presence in Greece, for one thing.) You can find them online.

Possible exam question or written assignment: You are the historian Polybius answering the Romans: why should Philopoemen's monuments remain?

Titus Flamininus

> "It is a very rare thing amongst men, to find a man very valiant, and wise withal: but yet of all sorts of valiant men, it is harder to find a just man."
> Plutarch, *Life of Titus Flamininus*

Introduction

Titus Quintius Flamininus was a consul and general of Rome, who lived from approximately 227 to 174 B.C. He is also called Titus Quinctius Flamininus, and Thomas North sometimes refers to him as "T. Quintius." Books and websites will sometimes refer to Plutarch's *Life of Titus*. (See the **Spelling** note as well.)

If you've done the previous study, Philopoemen, you've already met Titus Flamininus. If you haven't, I would suggest reading Plutarch's *Life of Philopoemen* first, so that you are familiar with the time period: the "old age" of ancient Greece and the rapid growth of the Roman Republic, around 200 B.C. In 146 B.C., Greece finally became a Roman province (called Athens); but Rome had been involved in Greek and Macedonian affairs before the final takeover.

Spelling

Flamininus (pronounced with a long I sound for the second I) is sometimes spelled **Flaminius** by early writers, including Thomas North. I have used "Flamininus" here, but the spelling issue is worth noting as it does come up both ways.

Who was Philip of Macedon?

It's important to get some dates straight, to be clear on which Philip fought against Titus Flamininus. Students may be familiar with Philip II, father of Alexander the Great, who ruled from 359 BC until his assassination in 336 BC. The King Philip in this story is Philip V, father of Perseus (studied in Plutarch's *Life of Aemilius Paulus*). He ruled from from 221 to 179 BC. In the passage for Lesson Four, North translates a phrase as "to make King Philip more famous in the world, than ever was Alexander his father," but it means more like "forefather." Dryden leaves it out altogether: "to make the name of Philip more glorious than that of Alexander."

Helpful Resources

I would suggest finding a map of ancient Greece to look at as you read. You will be looking for places such as Epirus, Thessaly, Chalcis, and Thebes.

If you are interested in reading about these events in a history book or encyclopedia, look under the First and Second Macedonian Wars.

Lesson One

Introduction

Do you think you could look at a class photograph and pick out the leaders of tomorrow? How would you choose?

Plutarch often starts out his *Lives* by giving someone's family story or the details of his childhood or education. Titus Flamininus is introduced as a young man going through the usual Roman military training—but with unusual speed and determination. By the time

Titus Flamininus

Tiitus was almost thirty, he had been elected to one of the top positions in the government of the Roman Republic.

Vocabulary

> **beholden to him:** owing him a debt
>
> **martial:** military
>
> **Hannibal:** General of Carthage; studied in Plutarch's Life of Fabius
>
> **Narnia and Cossa:** two cities that the Romans wanted to "inhabit" at that time. Narnia (also called Narni) was named after the river Nar. When C.S. Lewis was young, he saw "Narni" in an atlas, and remembered it later when he needed a name for his fictional land.
>
> **mean offices**: low positions
>
> **aedile, tribune, praetor, consul:** positions of increasing authority in the Roman Republic
>
> **the inferior offices of the commonwealth:** the lower positions of government
>
> **the Senate preferred it wholly to the voices of the people:** the Roman Senate let the citizens decide the matter with a vote
>
> **pronounced him consul openly, with Sextus Ælius:** two consuls were elected to serve together for one year at a time
>
> **it was all against themselves:** it would have been a mistake, they would have been acting against their interests
>
> **victuals:** food (for the army)
>
> **Howbeit that may more plainly appear, by declaring of his acts:** We will see that more clearly when we look at his actions.

Reading

It is easy to see Titus Quintius Flamininus' form, and stature, by Philopoemen's statue of brass, to whom we compare him: the which [*his statue*] is now set up at Rome, near to great Apollo that was brought from Carthage, and is placed right against the coming in to the showplace [*the Circus Maximus*], under which there is an inscription in Greek letters.

But for his nature and conditions, they say of him thus: he would quickly be angry, and yet very ready to pleasure men again. For, if he did punish any man that hath angered him, he would do it gently, but his anger did not long continue with him. He did good also to many, and ever loved them whom he had once pleasured, as if they had done him some pleasure: and was ready to do for them still whom he found thankful, because he would ever make them **beholden to him**, and thought that as honourable a thing, as he could purchase to himself, because he greatly sought honour above all things, when any notable service was to be done, he would do it himself, and no man should take it out of his hand. He would ever be rather with them that needed his help, than with those that could help him, or do him good. For, the first he esteemed as a mean[s] to exercise his virtue with: the other, he took them as his fellows and followers of honour with him.

He came to man's [e]state, when the city of Rome had greatest wars and trouble. At that time all the youth of Rome, which were of age to carry weapons, were sent to the wars to learn to trail the pike [basic training], and how to become good captains. Thus was he entered into **martial** affairs, and the first charge he took, was in the war against **Hannibal** of Carthage, where he was made colonel of a thousand footmen, under Marcellus the **consul**: who being slain by an ambush Hannibal had laid for him between the cities of Bancia, and Venusa, then they did choose Titus Quintius Flamininus governor of the province and city of Tarentum, which was now taken again the second time.

In this government of his, he won the reputation as much of a good and just man, as he did of an expert and skillful captain. By reason whereof, when the Romans were requested to send men to inhabit the cities of **Narnia and Cossa**, he was appointed the chief leader of them, which chiefly gave him heart and courage to aspire at the first to the consulship, passing over all other **mean offices**, as to be **aedile**, **tribune**, or **praetor**, by which (as by degrees) other young men were wont to attain the **consulship**. Therefore when the time came that the consuls should be elected, he did present himself among other[s], accompanied with a great number of those he had brought with him, to inhabit the two new towns, who did make earnest suit for him. But the two tribunes, Fulvius and Manlius, spake against him, and said: it was out of all reason, that so young a man should in such manner press to have the office of the highest dignity, against the use and custom of Rome, before he had passed through **the inferior offices of the commonwealth**. Nevertheless, **the Senate preferred it wholly to the voices of the people**: who presently **pronounced him consul openly**, with Sextus Ælius, although he was not yet thirty years old.

Afterwards, dividing the offices of the state by lot: it fell upon T. Quintius to make war with Philip king of Macedon. In the which methinks Fortune greatly favoured the Romans' affairs, that made such a man general of wars: for, to have [ap]pointed a general that by force and violence would have sought all things at the Macdonians' hands, that were a people to be won rather by gentleness and persuasions, than by force and compulsion: **it was all against themselves**. Philip, to maintain the brunt of a battle against the Romans, had power enough of his own in his realm of Macedon: but to make war any long time, to furnish himself with money and **victuals**, to have a place and cities to retire unto, and lastly, to have all other necessaries for his men and army: it stood him upon to get the force of Greece [to help him]. And had not the force of Greece been politically cut from him, the wars against him [would have] not been ended with one battle. Moreover, Greece (which never before bare the Romans any great goodwill) would not have dealt then so [quickly] in friendship with them, had not their general [Titus] been (as he was) a gentle person, lowly, and tractable, that won them more by his wisdom, than by his force, and could both eloquently utter his mind to them, and courteously also hear them speak, that had to do with him, and chiefly ministered justice and equity to every man alike. For it is not to be thought that Greece would otherwise so soon have withdrawn themselves from the rule of those with whom they were acquainted, and governed: and have put themselves under the rule of strangers, but that they saw great justice and lenity in them. **Howbeit that may more plainly appear, by declaring of his acts**.

Narration and Discussion

How was it that Titus rose so quickly through the Roman ranks, in fact jumping over most of the lower positions?

Why was Titus a fortunate choice to lead the Roman army against the Macedonians?

Lesson Two

Setting: The Battle of the Aous, 198 B.C.

Introduction

Imagine that you work for a big company, and that you've just been promoted to president, with your own secretary and a fancy private office. Since you're the president now, you have your choice of how you spend your days. Should you call a big company meeting with your bothersome board of directors; or stay in your office and order lunch? Go on a business trip to negotiate with someone who's ruthlessly taking over a lot of smaller companies (and who doesn't want you to interfere); or spend the week planning a party? Titus decided to take the active approach.

Who were the Ætolians?

Kings Philip and Antiochus may seem to have been the enemies of Titus, but if he had a real, ongoing collective enemy, it was the Ætolians. And yet they were not a race of evil monsters—just a confederation of unhappy Greeks.

(You don't have to use the Æ character; it is often just written Aetolia.)

Vocabulary

> **to take some strait, or to cut off victuals:** to capture a small passage or harass the other army; Titus thought these were rather puny achievements, "trifles."
>
> **their army by sea:** their navy

**to keep the strait and passage which is the entry into
Epirus:** Philip's army was guarding the passage or entry point to Epirus; Titus wanted to take control of it.

"very unhandsome for an army to pass that way, though they found not a man to keep the passage": Dryden translates this "not easily passable at any time for an army, but not at all when guarded by an enemy."

constrained: forced

neatherd: cowherd

the enemies kept not: the enemies left unguarded

he favoured them but underhand: he was friendly, but in secret

straitest: narrowest

so quietly, and with so great abstinence: without causing trouble or seizing food as they went (unusual behaviour for armies at the time)

unhandsome carriage thereof: the awkwardness of carrying it off

Reading

Titus was informed, that the generals before him [who had been] sent to the war in Macedon (as Sulpitius, and Publius Julius) used to come thither about the later end of the year, and made but cold wars, and certain light skirmishes, as sometime in one place, and sometime in another against Philip, and all **to take some strait, or to cut off victuals**: which he thought was not his way to follow their example. For they, tarrying at home, consumed the most of their consulship at Rome, in matters of government, and so enjoyed the honour of their office. Afterwards in the end of their year, they would set out to the wars, of intent to get another year over their heads in their office, that spending one year in their consulship at home, they might employ the other in the wars abroad. But Titus not minding to trifle out the half of his consulship at Rome, and the other abroad in the wars: did willingly leave all his honours and dignities he might have enjoyed by his office at Rome, and besought the Senate that they would appoint his brother Lucius Quintius lieutenant of **their army by sea**.

Furthermore, he took with himself about three thousand old soldiers of those that had first overthrown Asdrubal in Spain, and Hannibal afterwards in Africa, under the conduct of Scipio, which yet were able to serve, and were very willing to go with him in this journey, to be the strength of his army. With this company he passed the seas without danger, and landed in Epirus, where he found Publius Julius encamped with his army before King Philip, who of long time had lain in camp about the mouth of the river of Apsus, **to keep the strait and passage which is the entry into Epirus**. So that Publius Julius had lain still there, and done nothing, by reason of the natural force and hardness of the place. Then Titus took the army of him, and sent him to Rome.

Afterwards, [he] himself went in person to view and consider the nature of the country, which was in this sort. It is a long valley walled on either side with great high mountains, as those which shut in the valley of Tempe in Thessaly. Howbeit it had no such goodly woods, nor green forests, nor fair meadows, nor other like places of pleasure, as the other side had: but it was a great deep marsh or quagmire, through the midst whereof the river called Apsus did run, being in greatness and swiftness of stream, very like to the river of Peneus. The river did occupy all the ground at the feet of the mountains, saving a little way that was cut out of the main rock by man's hand, and a narrow straight path by the waterside, **very unhandsome for an army to pass that way, though they found not a man to keep the passage**.

There were some in the army that counselled Titus to fetch a great compass about by the country of Dassaretide, and by the city of Lyncus, where the country is very plain, and the way marvellous easy. Howbeit he stood in great fear he should lack victuals, if he stayed far from the sea, and happily if he fell into any barren or lean country, (Philip refusing the battle, and purposing to flee) he should be **constrained** in the end to return again towards the sea, without doing anything, as his predecessor had done before. Wherefore he determined to cross the mountains to set upon his enemy, and to prove if he could win the passage by force.

Now Philip kept the top of the mountains with his army, and when the Romans forced [their way] up the hills, they were received with darts, slings, and shot, that lighted amongst them here and there: insomuch as the skirmish was very hot for the time it lasted, and many were slain and hurt on either side. But this was not the end of the war.

For in the meantime there came certain **neatherds** of the country unto Titus (who did use to keep beasts on these mountains) and told him they could bring him a way which they knew **the enemies kept not**: by the which they promised to guide his army so, that in three days at the furthest, they would bring them on the top of the mountain. And because they might be assured that their words were true, they said they were sent to him by Charops, the son of Machatas. This Charops was the chiefest man of the Epirots, who loved the Romans very well, yet **he favoured them but underhand**, for fear of Philip. Titus gave credit unto them, and so sent one of his captains with them, with four thousand footmen, and three hundred horsemen. The herdmen that were their guides, went before still, fast bound: and the Romans followed after. All the day time the army rested in thick woods, and marched all night by moonlight, which was then by good hap at the full.

Titus, having sent these men away, rested all the rest of his camp: saving that some days he entertained them with some light skirmishes to occupy the enemy withal. But the same day, when his men that fetched a compass about, should come unto the top of the mountain above the camp of his enemies, he brought all his army out of the camp by break of day, and divided them into three troops. With the one of them he himself went on that side of the river where the way is **straitest**, making his bands to march directly against the side of the hill. The Macedonians again, they shot lustily at them from the height of the hill, and in certain places amongst the rocks they came to the sword. At the selfsame time, the two other troops on either hand of him did their endeavour likewise to get up the hill, and as it were envying one another, they climbed up with great courage against the sharp and steep hanging of the mountain.

When the sun was up, they might see afar off as it were, a certain smoke, not very bright at the beginning, much like to the mists we see commonly rise from the tops of the mountains. The enemies could see nothing, because it was behind them, and that the top of the mountain was possessed with the same. The Romans, though they were not assured of it, did hope being in the midst of the fight, that it was their fellows they looked for. But when they saw it increased still more, and more, and in such sort, that it darkened all the air: then they did assure themselves it was certainly the token their men did give them that they were come. Then they began to cry out, climbing up the hills with such a lusty courage, that they drave their enemies up the hill still, even unto the very rough and hardest places of the mountain. Their fellows also that were behind the enemies, did answer them with like loud cries from the top of the mountain: wherewith the enemies were so astoni[sh]ed, that they fled presently upon it. Nothwithstanding, there were not slain above two thousand of them, because the hardness and straitness of the place did so guard them, that they could not be chased.

But the Romans spoiled their camp, took all that they found in their tents, took also their slaves, and won the passage into the mountains, by the which they entered the country of Epirus: and did pass through it **so quietly, and with so great abstinence**, that though they were far from their ships and the sea, and lacked their ordinary portion of corn which they were wont to have monthly, and that victuals were very scant with them at that time, yet they never took anything of the country, though they found great store and plenty of all riches in it. For Titus was advertised, that Philip passing by Thessaly, and flying for fear, had caused the inhabitants of the cities to get them to the mountains, and then to set fire on their houses, and to leave those goods they could not carry away, by reason of the weight and **unhandsome carriage thereof**, to the spoil of his soldiers: and so (as it seemed) he left the whole country to the conquest of the Romans.

Whereupon Titus looking considerately to his doings, gave his men great charge to pass through the country without doing any hurt or mischief, as the same which their enemies had now left to them as their own.

Narration and Discussion

How did the Romans take the passage to Epirus? Give evidence that Titus was a different sort of general from those that had come before.

Discuss the conduct of the Roman soldiers under Titus. Why did he not allow them to rob or molest the civilians, although they did loot Philip's camp?

Lesson Three

Introduction

If you were told that your country was being invaded by barbarians, what would you expect them to look like? How would you expect them to act?

The Greeks were surprised when they met this young, well-mannered Roman general named Titus Flamininus, and they decided to trust him.

Who was Pyrrhus?

Pyrrhus was the king of Epirus from 307 to 302 B.C. and again from 295 to 272 B.C. He is the subject of Plutarch's *Life of Pyrrhus*.

Vocabulary

> **forbearing:** restraint, letting alone
>
> **he prayed audience:** he asked for the chance to speak publicly
>
> **prolong his time there:** give him authority to continue his "mission" in Greece (to lead the war against Macedon)
>
> **neither King Philip attained that he prayed:** Philip did not get what he wanted

Reading

So they tarried not long to enjoy the benefit of their orderly and wise **forbearing** of the country.

For, so soon as they were entered Thessaly, the cities willingly yielded themselves unto them: and the Grecians inhabiting beyond the country of Thermopyles, did marvellously desire to see Titus, asking no other thing, but to put themselves into his hands. The

Achaians also on the other side, did renounce the league and alliance they had made with Philip: and furthermore did determine in their council, to make war with him [Philip] on the Romans' side. And although the Ætolians were at that time friends and confederates with the Romans, and that they did shew themselves very loving to take their part in these wars: nevertheless when they desired the Opuntians that they would put their city into their hands, and were offered that it should be kept and defended from Philip: they would not hearken thereto, but sent for Titus, and put themselves and their goods wholly into his protection.

They say, that when King Pyrrhus first saw the Romans' army range in order of battle from the top of a hill, he said: This order of the barbarous people, setting of their men in battle [ar]ray, was not done in a barbarous manner. And those also that never had seen Titus before, and came for to speak with him: were compelled in a manner to say as much. For where they had heard the Macedonians say, that there came a captain of the barbarous people that destroyed all before him by force of arms, and subdued whole countries by violence: they said to the contrary, that they found him a man, indeed young of years, howbeit gentle, and courteous to look on, and that spake the Greek tongue excellently well, and was a lover only of true glory. By reason whereof they returned home marvellous glad, and filled all the cities and towns of Greece with goodwill towards him, and said: they had seen Titus the captain, that would restore them to their ancient liberty again. Then it much more appeared, when Philip shewed himself willing to have peace, and that Titus also did offer it him, and the friendship of the people of Rome, with these conditions: that he [Philip] would leave the Grecians their whole liberties, and remove his garrisons out of their cities and strongholds: which Philip refused to do. And thereupon all Greece, and even those which favoured Philip, said with one voice: that the Romans were not come to make wars with them, but rather with the Macedonians in favour of the Grecians. Whereupon all Greece came in, and offered themselves unto Titus without compulsion.

And as he passed through the country of Boeotia, without any shew at all of wars, the chiefest men of the city of Thebes went to meet him: who though they took part with [Philip] the king of Macedon, because of a private man called Brachylelis, yet they would honour Titus, as those which were contented to keep league and friendship with either side. Titus embraced them, and spake very courteously unto them, going on his way still fair and softly, entertaining them sometime with one matter, and sometime with another, and kept them [talking on purpose], to the end his soldiers being wearied with journeying, might in the meantime take good breath: and so marching on, by little and little, he entered into the city with them.

Wherewith the Lords of Thebes were not greatly pleased, but yet they durst not refuse him, though he had not at that time any number of soldiers about him. When he was within Thebes, **he prayed audience**, and began to persuade the people (as carefully as if he had not had the city already) that they would rather take part with the Romans, than with the king of Macedon.

And to further Titus' purpose, King Attalus being by chance at that time in the assembly, did help to exhort the Thebans very earnestly, that they would do as Titus persuaded them. But Attalus was more earnest than became a man of his years, for the desire he had (as was imagined) to shew Titus his eloquence: who did so strain and move himself withal, that he sounded suddenly in the midst of his oration, whereby the rheum fell down so fast upon him, that it took away his senses, so as he fell in a trance before them all, and few days after was conveyed again by sea into Asia, where he lived not long after. [*Dryden: And he, indeed, trying to play the advocate, beyond what it seems his age could bear, was seized, in the midst of his speech, with a sudden flux or dizziness, and swooned away; and, not long after, was conveyed by ship into Asia, and died there.*]

In the meantime, the Boeotians came into the Romans, and took their part. And Philip having sent ambassadors to Rome, Titus also sent thither [some] of his men to solicit for him, in two respects. The one, if wars continued against Philip, that then they would **prolong his time there**. The other, if the Senate did grant him peace: that they would do him the honour, as to make and conclude it with Philip. For Titus of his own nature being very ambitious, did fear lest they would send a successor to continue those wars, who should take the glory from him, and make an end of them. But his friends made such earnest suit for him, that **neither King Philip attained that he prayed**: neither was there sent any other general in Titus' place, but he still continued his charge in these wars.

Narration and Discussion

"A Greek in his voice and language, and a lover of honour." Explain what was meant by this.

Explain the situation with the men of Thebes. How did Titus deal with them?

Why did Titus want to continue the war, and more importantly, to continue to be at the center of it himself?

Lesson Four

Setting: The Battle of Cynoscephalae, 197 B.C.

Introduction

Philip of Macedon was now in Thessaly, and refused to leave the Greeks alone, so Titus marched out to fight him. The armies were equal in numbers, but the Macedonians discovered a problem with their famous phalanx formation: it only worked on level ground.

Vocabulary

- **the goodliest theater of the world:** "theater" is used in its military sense, meaning a large geographical area where military operations (battles etc.) are carried out.
- **charnel house:** crypt or burial mound: see Plutarch's explanation which follows
- **did of himself defer to give battle that day:** decided to hold off fighting
- **amain:** quickly, at full speed
- **unfurnished in many places:** sparsely guarded
- **sundered:** separated

which doth stay up one another: which support each other

Reading

Wherefore, so soon as he [Titus] had received his commission and authority from the Senate, he went straight towards Thessaly with great hope to overcome Philip. For he had in his army above six and twenty thousand fighting men, whereof the Ætolians made six thousand footmen, and three thousand horsemen. King Philip's army on the other side was no less in number, and they began to march one towards the other, until at the length they both drew near the city of Scotusa, where they determined to try the battle. So, neither they nor their men were afraid, to see themselves one so near another: but rather to the contrary, the Romans on the one side took greater heart and courage unto them, desiring to fight, as thinking with themselves what great honour they should win to overcome the Macedonians, who were so highly esteemed for their valiantness, by reason of the famous acts that Alexander the Great did by them. And the Macedonians on the other side also, taking the Romans for other manner of soldiers than the Persians, began to have good hope if they might win the field, to make King Philip more famous in the world, than ever was Alexander his father.

Titus then calling his men together, spake, and exhorted them to stand to it like men, and to show themselves valiant soldiers in this battle, as those which were to shew the proof of their valiantness in the heart of Greece: **the goodliest theater of the world**, and against their enemies of most noble fame. Philip then by chance, or forced to it by the speed he made, because they were both ready to join: did get up un[a]wares upon a **charnel house** (where they had buried many bodies, being a little hill raised up above the rest, and near the trenches of his camp), and there began to encourage his soldiers, as all generals do before they give battle. Who when he saw them all discouraged, for they took it for an ill sign that he was gotten up on the top of a grave to speak unto them: he of a conceit at the matter, **did of himself defer to give battle that day**.

The next morning, because the night was very wet by reason the south winds had blown, the clouds were turned to a mist, and filled all the valley with a dark gross thick air, coming from the mountains thereabouts, which covered the field between both camps with a mist all the morning: by reason whereof the scouts on both sides that were sent to discover what the enemies did, in very short time met together, and one gave charge upon another in a place they call the Dogs' Heads, which are points of rocks placed upon little hills one before another, and very near one unto another, which have been called so, because they have had some likeness of it. In this skirmish there were many changes, as commonly falleth out when they fight in such ill-favoured stony places. For sometime the Romans fled, and the Macedonians chased them: another time the Macedonians that followed the chase, were glad to fly themselves, and the Romans who fled before, now had them in chase. This change and alteration came, by sending new supplies still from both camps, to relieve them that were distressed and driven to flee.

Now began the mist to break up, and the air to clear, so that both generals might see about them what was done in either camp: by reason whereof both of them drew on their army to the field and battle. So Philip had the vantage on the right wing of his army, which was placed on the height of an hanging hill, from which they came so **amain** to set upon the Romans, and with such a fury, that the strongest and valiantest that could be, had never been able to abide the front of their battle, so closely were they joined together, and their wall of pikes was so strong. But on his left wing it was not so, because the ranks of his battle could not join so near, nor close target to target, the place being betwixt the hills and the rocks where the battle was coming, so as they were compelled by reason of the straitness and unevenness of the ground, to leave it open, and **unfurnished in many places**.

Titus finding that disadvantage, went from the left wing of his battle which he saw overlaid by the right wing of his enemies, and going suddenly toward the left wing of King Philip's battle, he set upon the Macedonians on that side, where he saw they could not close their ranks in the front, nor join them together in the midst of the battle (which is the whole strength and order of the Macedonian fight) because the field was uphill and downhill: and to fight hand to hand they were so pestered behind, that one thronged and overlaid another. For the battle of the Macedonians hath this property, that so long as the order is kept close and joined together, it seemeth as it were but the body of a beast of a force invincible. But also after that it is once open, and that they are **sundered** and not joined together, it doth not only lose the force and power of the whole body, but also of every private soldier that fighteth: partly by reason of the diversity of the weapons wherewith they fight, and partly for that their whole strength consisteth most, in the disposing and joining together of their ranks and orders **which doth stay up one another**, more than doth every private soldier's strength.

So when this left wing of the Macedonians was broken, and that they ran their way: one part of the Romans followed the chase, and the other ran to give a charge upon the flanks of the right wing which fought yet, and they made great slaughter of them.

Narration and Discussion

Why is it that "neither they nor their men were afraid, to see themselves one so near another?"

Compare the speeches that Titus and Philip made.

Consider the description of the phalanx. "For the battle of the Macedonians hath this property, that so long as the order is kept close and joined together, it seemeth as it were but the body of a beast of a force invincible. But also after that it is once open, and that they are sundered and not joined together, it doth not only lose the force and power of the whole body, but also of every private soldier that fighteth: partly by reason of the diversity of the weapons wherewith they fight, and partly for that their whole strength consisteth most, in the disposing and joining together of their ranks and orders which doth stay up one another, more than doth every private soldier's strength." Dryden translates this as ". . . irresistible so long as it is embodied into one, and keeps its order, shield touching shield, all as in a piece; but if it be once broken, not only is the joint-force lost, but the individual soldiers also who composed it, lose each one his own single strength, because of the nature of their armour; and because each of them is strong, rather, as he makes a part of the whole, than in himself." Do you see any similarity to the Body of Christ?

Lesson Five

Introduction

Who really won the battle?

And what would you do if you really, really wanted to annoy Titus?

Vocabulary

> **And had not the fault been in the Ætolians, Philip had not saved himself by flying as he did:** the Ætolians were blamed for letting Philip get away (because they were busy looting)
>
> **tarried:** lingered too long
>
> **without making account of…:** without including them in his plans

Reading

Whereupon they now which before had the vantage [*the Macedonians who had been in a better position to fight*], began to stagger and break, and in the end ran away as fast as the other [*Macedonians*] did, throwing down their weapons: insomuch as there were slain of them eight thousand in the field, and five thousand taken prisoners in the chase.

And had not the fault been in the Ætolians, Philip had not saved himself by flying as he did. For whilst the Romans had their enemies in chase, the Ætolians **tarried**, and rifled all King Philip's camp, so as they had left the Romans nothing to spoil at their return. Whereupon there grew great quarrel, and hot words between them, and one with another. But afterwards they angered Titus worse, challenging the honour of this victory to themselves, because they gave it out through Greece, that they alone had overthrown King Philip in the battle.

So that in the songs and ballads the poets made in praise of this victory, which every country and townsman had in his mouth: they always put the Ætolians before the Romans, as in this that followeth, which was currently sung in every place:

> Oh friend, which passest by: here lie we wretched fears
> Without honour of the grave, without lamenting tears.
> We thirty thousand were, which ended have our days:
> In cruel coasts of Thessaly, which caused our decays.
> We have been overthrown by the Ætolians' men of war:
> And by the Latin crews likewise, whom Titus led from far.
> Even out of Italy, to Macedonie land,
> Us to destroy, he (captain like) did come with mighty band.
> And Philip stout...for all his proud fierce face:
> Is fled more swift than hearts do run which are pursued in chase.
>
> [*Dryden's translation:*
> "Naked and tombless see, O passer-by,
> The thirty thousand men of Thessaly,
> Slain by the Aetolians and the Latin band,
> That came with Titus from Italia's land;
> Alas for mighty Macedon! that day,
> Swift as a roe, King Philip fled away."]

The Poet was Alcæus that made these verses for to sing, who did them in disgrace of King Philip, falsely increasing the number of his men which died in the battle, only to shame and spite him the more: howbeit he spited Titus thereby, more than Philip, because it was sung in every place.

For Philip laughed at it, and to encounter him again with the like mock, he made a song to counterfeit his, as followeth:

> This gibbet on this hill which passersby may mark:
> Was set to hang Alcæus up, withouten leaves or bark.
>
> [*Dryden*: "Naked and leafless see, O passer-by,
> The cross that shall Alcæus crucify."]

But Titus took it grievously, who chiefly desired to be honoured amongst the Grecians, by reason whereof from that time forwards he dealt in the rest of his matters alone, **without making account of the Ætolians**: wherewith they were marvellous angry, and specially when he received an ambassador from Philip, and gave ear unto a treaty of peace which he offered. For then they were so nettled against him, that they gave it out through all Greece, that Titus had sold peace unto Philip, when he might altogether have ended the war, and utterly have destroyed Philip's whole power and empire, who had first brought Greece into bondage. These slanderous reports and false tales which the Ætolians spread thus abroad, did much trouble the Romans' friends and confederates: but Philip [him]self pulled this suspicion out of their heads, when he came in person to require peace, and did submit himself wholly to the discretion of Titus and the Romans.

Narration and Discussion

"The Poet was Alcæus that made these verses for to sing, who did them in disgrace of King Philip, falsely increasing the number of his men which died in the battle, only to shame and spite him the more: howbeit he spited Titus thereby, more than Philip, because it was sung in every place." Why did the verses cause more "spite" against Titus than they did against Philip? (Writing idea: write an "elegiac verse" that Titus might have composed about the Ætolians.)

"For then they were so nettled against him, that they gave it out through all Greece, that Titus had sold peace unto Philip, when he might altogether have ended the war, and utterly have destroyed Philip's whole power and empire, who had first brought Greece into bondage." Was this true?

Lesson Six

Introduction

The Greeks seemed somewhat puzzled about what the Roman victory meant for them, and things weren't helped by the constant agitations of the Ætolians.

Vocabulary

>**Antiochus:** Antiochus II (the Great) of Syria; reigned 223-187 B.C.
>
>**whom he put in the head:** to whom he suggested
>
>**with good garrison:** keeping a Roman military presence (a fort) there

delivered from garrison: having the fort and soldiers removed from those cities

bruit and tumult: noise and confusion

in such audible wise: so loudly

letting the games alone: forgetting about the sports

void: empty

betimes: in good time, early

Reading

Titus then granted him [Philip] peace, and delivered to him his realm of Macedon, and commanded him he should give over all that he held in Greece, and besides, that he should pay one thousand talents for tribute, taking from him all his army by sea, saving only ten ships: and for assurance of this peace, he took one of his sons for hostage, whom he sent to Rome. Wherein Titus certainly did very well, and wisely did foresee the time to come.

For then Hannibal of Carthage, (the great enemy of the Romans) was banished out of his country, and came to King **Antiochus, whom he put in the head**, and earnestly moved, to follow his good fortune, and the increase of his Empire. Whom Hannibal so followed with these persuasions, that King Antiochus at length was come to it. And trusting to his former good success, and notable acts, whereby in the wars before he had attained the surname of Great: he began now to aspire to the monarchy of the whole world, and sought how to find occasion to make wars with the Romans.

So that if Titus (foreseeing that afar off) had not wisely inclined to peace, but that the wars of Antiochus had fallen out together with the wars of King Philip, and that these two, the mightiest princes of the world, had joined together against the city of Rome: then it had been in as great trouble and danger, as ever it was before, in the time of their wars against Hannibal. Howbeit Titus having haply thrust in this peace between both wars, he cut off the war that was present, before the other that was coming: by which means he took from one of the kings his last, and from the other his first hope. In the meantime, the ten commissioners that were sent by the Senate from Rome to Titus, to aid and assist him in the order of the affairs of Greece: did counsel him to set all the rest of Greece at liberty, and only to keep in their hands **with good garrison**, the cities of Chalcide, of Corinth, and of Demetriade, to make sure that by practise they should not enter into league and alliance with Antiochus.

Then the Ætolians (that were the common slanderers of Titus' proceedings) began openly to make these cities to rebel, and did summon Titus to loose the chains of Greece: for so did King Philip call these three cities. Then they asked the Grecians in mockery, whether they were willing now to have heavier fetters on their legs, than before, being somewhat brighter and fairer than those they had been shackled with: and also whether they were not greatly behold[en] to Titus for taking of the fetters from the Grecians' legs, and tying them about their necks. Titus being marvellously troubled and vexed with this, moved the ten counsellors so earnestly, that he made them grant his request in the end, that those three cities also should be **delivered from garrison**: because the Grecians thenceforth might no more complain, that his grace and liberality was not thoroughly performed, and accomplished in every respect on them all.

Wherefore, when the feast called Isthmia was come, there were gathered together an infinite multitude of people come to see the sport of the games played there: for Greece having been long time troubled with wars, they seeing themselves now in sure peace, and in very good hope of full liberty, looked after no other thing, but delighted only to see games, and to make merry. Proclamation was then made by sound of trumpet in the assembly, that every man should keep silence. That done, the herald went forward, and thrust into the midst of the multitude, and proclaimed out aloud: That the Senate of Rome, and Titus Quintius Flamininus, consul of the people of Rome (now that they had overthrown King Philip and the Macedonians in battle) did thenceforth discharge from all garrisons, and set at liberty from all taxes, subsidies, and impositions for ever, to live after their old ancient laws, and in full liberty: the Corinthians, the Locrians, those of Phocide, those of the Isle of Euboea, the Achaians, the Phthiotes, the Magnesians, the Thessalians, and the Perrhaebeians.

At the first time of the proclamation, all the people could not hear the voice of the herald, and the most part of those that heard him, could not tell distinctly what he said: for there ran up and down the showplace where the games were played, a confused **bruit and tumult** of the people that wondered, and asked what the matter meant, so as the herald was driven again to make the proclamation.

Whereupon after silence made, the herald putting out his voice far louder than before, did proclaim it **in such audible wise**, that the whole assembly heard him: and then rose there such a loud shout and cry of joy through the whole people, that the sound of it was heard to the sea. Then all the people that had taken their places, and were set to see the swordplayers play, rose up all on their feet, **letting the games alone**, and went together with great joy to salute, to embrace, and to thank Titus the recoverer, protector, and patron of all their liberties of Greece.

Then was seen (which is much spoken of) the power of men's voices: for crows fell down at that present time among the people, which by chance flew over the show place at that time that they made the same out-shout. This came to pass, by reason the air was broken and cut asunder, with the vehemency and strength of the voices, so as it had not his natural power in it, to keep up the flying of the birds: which were driven of necessity to fall to the ground, as flying through a **void** place where they lacked air. Unless we will rather say, that it was the violence of the cry, which struck the birds passing through the air, as they had been hit with arrows, and so made them fall down dead to the earth. It may be also, that there was some hurling wind in the air, as we do see sometime in the sea, when it riseth high, and many times turneth about the waves, by violence of the storm. So it is, that if Titus had not prevented the whole multitude of people which came to see him, and that he had not got him away **betimes**, before the games were ended: he [would have] hardly [e]scaped from being stifled amongst them, the people came so thick about him from every place. But after that they were weary of crying, and singing about his pavilion until night, in the end they went their way: and as they went, if they met any of their kin, friends or citizens, they did kiss and embrace one another for joy, and so supped, and made merry together.

In their more rejoicing yet, as we may think full well, they had no other talk at the table, but of the wars of Greece, discoursing amongst them what sundry great wars they had made, what they had endured heretofore, and all to defend and recover their liberty. And yet for all that, they could never so joyfully nor more assuredly obtain it, than they did even at that present, receiving the honourablest reward, and that which deserved greatest fame through the world: that by the valiantness of strangers who fought for the same (without any spilt blood of their own in comparison, or that they lost the life of any one man, whose death they had cause to lament) they were so restored to their ancient freedom and liberty.

Narration and Discussion

Explain why it was so important for Titus to make peace with Philip right then.

The Greeks were asked "whether they were willing now to have heavier fetters on their legs, than before, being somewhat brighter and fairer than those they had been shackled with . . ." Dryden translates it "whether it were not matter of much consolation to them, that, though their chains weighed heavier, yet they were now smoother and better polished than formerly." Is that a fair description of life under Roman rule? If you had to be "chained," which would you prefer?

Something to think about: why was it hard for Titus to see Roman rule from that perspective? What kind of image might he have preferred to use? What did he do to prove that (from his viewpoint) he really did have the best interests of Greece at heart?

Lesson Seven

Introduction

Titus continued to dismantle the Macedonian fortifications, and to act as the "liberator" of Greece.

Vocabulary

fell out against themselves: decreased their power more than they helped; came back to bite them later. Dryden says, "Greece fought all her battles against, and to enslave, herself."

a strange nation: a foreign nation

at one self time: all at once

out of the which he took all the garrisons of the cities: he removed the enemy forts

judge and rector of the games: the one who presides over them

Zenocrates: Xenocrates of Chalcedon, who lived from c. 396-314 B.C. This story is given to show the benefits of mercy, not as something that happened during the life of Flamininus.

Reading

It is a very rare thing amongst men, to find a man very valiant, and wise withal: but yet of all sorts of valiant men, it is harder to find a just man. For Agesilaus, Lysander, Nicias, Alcibiades, and all other the famous captains of former times, had very good skill to lead an army, and to win the battle, as well by sea as by land: but to turn their victories to any honourable benefit, or true honour among men, they could never skill of it. And if you do except the battle against the barbarous people in the plain of Marathon, the battle of Salamina [*Salamis*], the journey of Plataes, the battle of Thermopyles, the battle Cimon fought about Cyprus, and upon the river of Eurymedon: all the other wars and battles of Greece that were made, **fell out against themselves**, and did ever bring them into bondage: and all the tokens of triumph which ever were set up for the same, was to their shame and loss. So that in the end, Greece was utterly destroyed and overthrown, and that chiefly through the wickedness and self will of her governors and captains of the cities, one envying another's doing. Where[as] **a strange nation**, the which (as it should seem) had very small occasion to move them to do it (for that they have had no great familiarity with ancient Greece, and through the counsel and good wisdom of the which it should seem very strange that Greece could receive any benefit) have notwithstanding with dangerous battles and infinite troubles, delivered it from oppression, and servitude, of violent lords and tyrants.

This, and such like talk, did at that time occupy the Grecians' heads: and moreover, the deeds following did answer and perform the words of the proclamation. For **at one self time**, Titus sent Lentulus into Asia, to set the Bargylians at liberty, and Titillius into Thracia, to remove the garrisons out of the isles and cities which Philip had kept there: and Publius Julius was sent also into Asia, unto King Antiochus, to speak unto him to set the Grecians at liberty which he kept in subjection. And as for Titus, he went himself unto the city of Chalcide [Chalcis], where he took sea, and went into the province of Magnesia, **out of the which he took all the garrisons of the cities**, and redelivered the government of the commonwealth unto the citizens of the same.

Afterwards when time came, that the feast of Nemea was celebrated in the city of Argos in the honour of Hercules, Titus was chosen **judge and rector of the games** that were played there: where, after he had set all things in very good order, pertaining unto the solemnity of the feast, he caused again solemn proclamation to be made openly, for the general liberty of all Greece. Furthermore, visiting the cities, he did [e]stablish very good laws, reformed justice, and did set the inhabitants and citizens of every one of them in good peace, amity, and concord one with another: and did call home also all those that were outlaws and banished men, and pacified all old quarrels and dissensions among them. The which did no less please and content him, that by persuasions he could bring the Grecians to be reconciled one with the other: than if he had by force of arms overcome the Macedonians. Insomuch, as the recovery of the liberty which Titus had restored unto the Grecians, seemed unto them the least part of the goodness they had received at his hands.

They say, that Lycurgus the orator, seeing the collectors of taxes carry **Zenocrates** the Philosopher one day to prison, for lack of payment of a certain imposition, which the strangers inhabiting within the city of Athens were to pay: he rescued him from them by force, and moreover prosecuted law so hard against them, that he made them pay a fine for the injury they had done unto so worthy a person. And they tell, how the same philosopher afterwards meeting Lycurgus' children in the city, said unto them: I do well requite your father's good turn he did me: for I am the cause that he is praised and commended of every man, for the kindness he shewed on my behalf.

Titus Flamininus

So the good deeds of the Romans, and of Titus Quintius Flamininus unto the Grecians, did not only reap this benefit unto them, in recompense that they were praised and honoured of all the world: but they were cause also of increasing their dominions and empire over all nations, and that the world afterwards had great affiance and trust in them, and that most justly. So that the people and cities [*of Greece*] did not only receive the captains and governors the Romans sent them: but they also went to Rome unto them, and procured them to come, and did put themselves into their hands. And not only the cities and communalities, but kings and princes also (which were oppressed by others more mighty than themselves) had no other refuge, but to put themselves under their [*Roman*] protection: by reason whereof in a very short time (with the favour and help of the gods as I am persuaded) all the world came to submit themselves to their obedience, and under the protection of their Empire.

Narration and Discussion

Discuss these sentences:

"It is a very rare thing amongst men, to find a man very valiant, and wise withal: but yet of all sorts of valiant men, it is harder to find a just man."

"So that in the end, Greece was utterly destroyed and overthrown, and that chiefly through the wickedness and self will of her governors and captains of the cities, one envying another's doing."

Would you say that the Greeks' newfound trust in Titus (or in Rome) was wise, or were they taken in? Did they have any choice? (Does Plutarch go a bit overboard in praising Rome here?)

Lesson Eight

Introduction

Before you start, review what you know of Titus so far. What key words characterize his personality and his leadership?

In this passage, Titus engaged in "a goodly and just war against Nabis, the cursed and wicked tyrant of Lacedaemon." (Obviously Plutarch was not planning on writing a *Life of Nabis*.)

Vocabulary

Lacedaemon: Sparta

Philopoemen: see Plutarch's *Life of Philopoemen*

contentation: satisfaction

Titus' suit and intercession: the influence and persuasion of Titus

Reading

Titus also did glory more, that he had restored Greece again unto liberty, than in any other service or exploit he had ever done. For when he offered up unto the temple of Apollo in the city of Delphes [*Delphi*], the targets of silver with his own shield, he made these verses to be graven upon them, in effect as followeth:

> O noble twins Tyndarides, Dan Jove his children dear:
> Throw out loud shouts of joy and mirth, rejoice and make good cheer.
> O noble kings of Spartan soil, which take delight to ride
> Your trampling steeds, with foamy bit, and trappings by their side:
> Rejoice you now, for Titus, he, the valiant Roman knight,
> These gifts so great to you hath got, even by his force and might.
> That having taken clean away from off the Greekish necks
> The heavy yoke of servitude, which held them thrall to cheeks,
> Unto their former liberty he hath restored them free,
> Which altogether perished was, as men might plainly see.
>
> [*Dryden's version:*
> "Ye Spartan Tyndarids, twin sons of Jove,
> Who in swift horsemanship have placed your love,

> Titus, of great Aeneas's race, leaves this
> In honour of the liberty of Greece."]

He gave a crown of massy gold unto Apollo, upon the which he made this inscription to be written:

> A valiant Roman knight, even Titus by his name,
> A captain worthy by desert, of high renown and fame:
> To thee (Apollo god) this crown of pure fine gold
> Hath given thy godhead to adorn, with jewels manifold.
> Therefore let it thee please (Apollo god of grace).
> With favour to requite this love to him and to his face:
> That his renowned fame and virtue may be spread,
> And blazed through the world so wide, to shew what life he led.
>
> [*Dryden:*
> This golden crown upon thy locks divine,
> O blest Latonia's son, was set to shine
> By the great captain of the Aenean name.
> O Phoebus, grant the noble Titus fame!]

So hath the city of Corinth enjoyed this good hap, that the Grecians have been twice proclaimed to be set at liberty: the first time by Titus Quintius Flamininus, and the second time, by Nero in our time, and [*both*] at the selfsame instant when they solemnly kept the feast called Isthmia. Howbeit the first proclamation of their liberty (as we have told ye before) was done by the voice of a herald: and the second time it was done by Nero himself, who proclaimed it in an oration he made unto the people in open assembly, in the marketplace of the city of Corinth. But it was a long time after.

Furthermore, Titus began then a goodly and just war against Nabis, the cursed and wicked tyrant of **Lacedaemon**. Howbeit in the end he deceived the expectation of Greece. For when he might have taken him, he would not do it, but made peace with him, forsaking poor Sparta unworthily oppressed under the yoke of bondage: either because he was afraid that if the war held on, there should come a successor unto him from Rome, that tyrant should carry the glory away to end the same, or else he stood jealous and envious of the honour they did unto **Philopoemen**. Who having shewed himself in every place as excellent a captain as ever came in Greece, and having done notable acts and famous service, both of great wisdom, and also of valiantness, and specially in the Achaians' war, he was as much honoured and reverenced of the Achaians, in the theaters and common assemblies, even as Titus was. Whereat Titus was marvellously offended, for he thought it unreasonable, that an Arcadian who had never been general of an army, but in small little wars against his neighbours, should be as much esteemed and honoured, as a consul of Rome, that was come to make wars for the recovery of the liberty of Greece. But Titus alleged reasonable excuse for his doings, saying that he saw very well he could not destroy this tyrant Nabis, without the great loss and misery of the other Spartans.

Furthermore, of all the honours the Achaians ever did him (which were very great) methinks there was none that came near any recompense of his honourable and well deserving, but one only present they offered him, and which he above all the rest most esteemed: and this it was. During the second wars of Africa, which the Romans had against Hannibal, many Romans were taken prisoners in the sundry battles they lost, and being sold here and there, remained slaves in many countries: and amongst other[s], there were dispersed in Greece to the number of twelve hundred, which from time to time did move men with pity and compassion towards them, that saw them in so miserable change and state of fortune. But then much more was their misery to be pitied, when these captives found in the Romans' army, some of them their sons, other their brethren, and the rest their fellows and friends, free, and conquerors, and themselves slaves and bondmen. It grieved Titus much to see these poor men in such miserable captivity, notwithstanding he would not take them by force from those that had them. Whereupon the Achaians redeemed and bought them for five hundred pence a man, and having gathered them together into a troop, they presented all the Roman captives unto Titus, even as he was ready to take ship to return into Italy: which present made him return home with greater joy and **contentation**, having received for his noble deeds so honourable a recompense, and worthy of himself, that was so loving a man to his citizens and country.

And surely, that only was the ornament (in my opinion) that did most beautify his triumph. For these poor redeemed captives did that, which the slaves are wont to do on that day when they be set at liberty: to wit, they shave their heads, and do wear little hats upon them. The Romans that were thus redeemed, did in like manner: and so followed Titus' chariot, on the day of his triumph and entry made into Rome in the triumphing manner.

It was a goodly sight also, to see the spoils of the enemies, which were carried in the show of this triumph: as, store of helmets after the Grecians' fashion, heaps of targets, shields, and pikes after the Macedonian manner, with a wonderful sum of gold and silver. For Itanus the historiographer writeth, that there was brought a marvellous great mass of treasure in nuggets of gold, of three thousand seven hundred and thirteen pound weight, and of silver, of forty three thousand, two hundred, three score and ten pound weight, and of gold ready coined in pieces called "Philips" fourteen thousand, five hundred, and fourteen, besides the thousand talents King Philip should pay for a ransom. The which sum, the Romans afterwards forgave him, chiefly at **Titus' suit and intercession**, who procured that grace for him, and caused him to be called a friend and confederate of the people of Rome, and his son Demetrius to be sent unto him again, who remained before as an hostage at Rome.

Narration and Discussion

The big question here: why did Titus let Nabis go and make peace with him instead of destroying him? What are the three possible reasons that Plutarch suggests?

Sometimes we can't seem to get enough of the things we want most. Some people crave thrills and excitement to the point that even hang gliding becomes boring. Some people will do almost anything for love and affection. What is it that Titus just couldn't get enough of? How could that desire begin to be a problem for him?

Lesson Nine

Introduction

Antiochus of Syria (aided by the Ætolians) arrived in Greece, trying to stir things up against Rome, and to liberate the Greeks from their liberators. Titus was not consul at this point, but he returned as lieutenant to the current consul. His presence seemed to ease some of the tension, reminding the Greeks of the trust they had established. ("If you won't do it for Rome, at least do it for Titus.")

Vocabulary

Thermopyles, Thermopylae: not the famous battle of 480 B.C. with the Greeks vs. the Persians; this battle at Thermopylae was fought by the Romans against Syria

puissant: powerful

"but for that they had no just cause to make war, they taught him to cloak it the honestest way he could": Dryden translates this "in lack of really honourable grounds, he was instructed to employ these lofty professions."

Manius Acilius: Manius Acilius Glabrio was a consul of the Roman Republic in 191 B.C.

to flee out, and to shrink into Greece, from them: to escape the situation (and the Romans)

physic: medicine

being overcome in the country of Thermopyles: having lost this later battle of Thermopylae

Reading

Shortly after, King Antiochus went out of Asia into Greece with a great fleet of ships, and a very **puissant** army, to stir up the cities to forsake their league and alliance with the Romans, and to make a dissension amongst them. To further this his desire and enterprise, the Ætolians did aid and back him, which of long time had borne great and secret malice against the Romans, and desired much to have had wars with them. So they taught King Antiochus to say, that the war which he took in hand, was to set the Grecians at liberty, whereof they had no need, because they did already enjoy their liberty: **but for that they had no just cause to make war, they taught him to cloak it the honestest way he could.**

Wherefore the Romans fearing greatly the rising of the people, and the rumour of the power of this great king, they sent thither **Manius Acilius** their general, and Titus, [acting as] one of his lieutenants, for the Grecians' sakes. Which arrival did the more assure them that already bare good will to the Romans, after they had once seen Manius and Titus; and the rest that began **to flee out, and to shrink into Greece, from them**, those Titus kept in obedience from starting, remembering them of the friendship and goodwill they had borne him, even like a good skilful physician that could give his patient **physic** to preserve him from a contagious disease. Indeed there were some (but few of them) that left him, which were won and corrupted before by the Ætolians: and though he had just cause of offence towards them, yet he saved them after the battle. For King Antiochus **being overcome in the country of Thermopyles**, fled his way, and in great haste took the sea to return into Asia.

And the consul Manius following his victory, entered into the country of the Ætolians, where he took certain towns by force, and left the other for a prey unto King Philip. So Philip king of Macedon on the one side, spoiled and sacked the Dolopians, the Magnesians, the Athamanians, and the Aperantines: and the consul Manius on the other side, destroyed the city of Heraclea, and laid siege to the city of Naupactum, which the Ætolians kept. But Titus taking compassion of them, to see the poor people of Greece thus spoiled and turned out of all: went out of Peloponnesus (where he was then) unto **Manius Acilius'** camp, and there reproved him for suffering King Philip to usurp the benefit and reward of his honourable victory, still conquering many people, kings, and countries, whilst he continued siege before a city, and only to wreak his anger upon them. Afterwards, when they that were besieged saw Titus from their walls, they called him by his name, and held up their hands unto him, praying him he would take pity upon them: but he gave them never a word at that time, and turning his back unto them, he fell a-weeping.

Afterwards he spake with Manius, and appeasing his anger, got him to grant the Ætolians truce for certain days, in which time they might send ambassadors to Rome, to see if they could obtain grace and pardon of the Senate.

Narration and Discussion

What kind of a role did Titus have during this time when he had been replaced as consul? Can you see any signs that his being out of office bothered him?

How did Titus show compassion (magnanimity) for Greece, and especially for the Ætolians, after the defeat of Antiochus at Thermopylae? Was this unexpected?

Why did Titus turn his back on those who were besieged?

Lesson Ten

Introduction

In this passage we have examples both of the honour shown to Titus, and of his ironic sense of humour. (This was a high point for Titus: the last two lessons take a slightly different turn.)

Vocabulary

> **the Chalcidians were much affected unto King Antiochus**: Dryden translates this, "The Chalcidians, in consequence, embraced the king's interests with zeal and alacrity . . ."

> **passing fair:** quite pretty

> **lie upon him:** try to coax him

> **superscriptions:** inscriptions written over the doors

> **feignedly:** insincerely

> **for emulation of honour:** desiring the most honoured place

> **but he ever ended the heat of his words, in council and assemblies, where he uttered his mind frankly to them both:** Dryden's translation: "but when it had vented itself in some citizen-like freedom of speech, there was an end of it."

parled: spoke

and did number them by many diverse names: Dryden translates this "a long catalogue of hard names."

Reading

But the most trouble and difficulty he had, was to entreat for the Chalcidians, with whom the Consul Manius was more grievously offended, than with all the rest: because that King Antiochus, after the war was begun, had married his wife in their city, when he was past years of marriage, and out of all due time. For he was now very old, and in the midst of his wars, he fell in [love] with a young gentlewoman, the daughter of Cleoptolemus, the fairest woman that was at that time in all Greece. Therefore **the Chalcidians were much affected unto King Antiochus**, and did put their city into his hands, to serve him in this war, for a strong and safe retiring place.

Whereupon, when Antiochus had lost the battle [*at Thermopylae*], he came thither [*to Chalcide, or Chalcis*] with all possible speed, and taking from thence with him his **passing fair** young queen which he had married, and his gold, his silver, and friends, he took the seas incontinently, and returned into Asia.

For this cause the consul Manius, having won the battle, did march straight with his army towards the city of Chalcide in a great rage and fury. But Titus that followed him, did always **lie upon him** to pacify his anger, and did so much entreat him, together with the other Romans of state and authority in council: that in the end, he got him to pardon them of Chalcide also.

Who, because they were preserved from peril by his means, they, to recompense this fact of his, did consecrate unto him, all their most stately and sumptuous buildinges and common works in their city, as appeareth yet by the **superscriptions** remaining to be seen at this day. As in the showplace of exercises: The people of Chalcide did dedicate this showplace of exercises. unto Titus and Hercules. And in the temple called Delphinium: The people of Chalcide did consecrate this temple unto Titus, and unto Apollo. And furthermore, unto this present time, there is a priest chosen by the voice of the people, purposely to do sacrifice unto Titus: in which sacrifice, after that the thing sacrificed is offered up, and wine poured upon it, the people standing by, do sing a song of triumph made in praise of him. But because it were too long to write it all out, we have only drawn in brief the latter end of the same: and this it is:

> The clear unspotted faith, of Romans we adore.
> And vow to be their faithful friends, both now and ever more.
> Sing out you Muses nine, to love's eternal fame.
> Sing out the honour due to Rome, and Titus' worthy name.
> Sing out (I say) the praise, of Titus and his faith:
> By whom you have preserved been, from ruin, dole, and death.

> [*Dryden's translation:*
> "The Roman Faith, whose aid of yore
> Our vows were offered to implore,
> We worship now and evermore.
> To Rome, to Titus, and to Jove,
> O maidens, in the dances move.
> Dances and Io-Paeans too
> Unto the Roman Faith are due,
> O Saviour Titus, and to you."]

Now the Chalcidians did not alone only honour and reverence Titus, but he was generally honoured also by the Grecians as he deserved, and was marvellously beloved for his courtesy and good nature: which argueth plainly that they did not **feignedly** honour him, or through compulsion, but even from the heart. For though there was some jar betwixt him and Philopoemen at the first about service, **for emulation of honour**, and after betwixt him and Diophanes also, both generals of the Achaians: yet he never bare them any malice in his heart, neither did his anger move him at any time to hurt them any way, **but he ever ended the heat of his words, in council and assemblies, where he uttered his mind frankly to them both**.

Therefore none thought him ever a cruel man, or eager of revenge: but many have thought him rash, and hasty of nature. Otherwise, he was as good a companion in company as possibly could be, and would use as pleasant wise mirth as any man.

[*Here are some stories about Titus's sense of humour.*] As when he said to the Achaians, on a time, who would needs unjustly usurp the isle of the Zacynthians, to dissuade them from it: My Lords of Achaia, if ye once go out of Peloponnesus, you put yourselves in danger, as the tortoises do, when they thrust their heads out of their shell. And the first time he **parled** with Philip to treat of peace: when Philip said unto him, you have brought many men with you, and I am come alone. Indeed it is true you are alone, said [Titus], because you made all your friends and kin to be slain.

In the council of the Achaians, King Antiochus' ambassadors being come thither, to move them to break their league with the Romans, and to make alliance with the king their master, they made a marvellous large discourse of the great multitude of soldiers that were in their master's army, **and did number them by many diverse names**. Whereunto Titus answered, and told how a friend of his having bidden him one night to supper, and having served so many dishes to his board, as he was angry with him for bestowing so great cost upon him, as wondering how he could so suddenly get so much store of meat, and of so diverse kinds. My friend said to me again, that all was but pork dressed so many ways, and with so sundry sauces. And even so (quoth Titus) my Lords of Achaia, esteem not King Antiochus' army the more, to hear of so many men of arms, numbered with their lances, and of such a number of footmen with their pikes: for they are all but Syrians, diversely armed, only with ill favoured little weapons.

Narration and Discussion

"But Titus that followed him, did always lie upon him to pacify his anger, and did so much entreat him, together with the other Romans of state and authority in council: that in the end, he got him to pardon them of Chalcide also." Why did Titus care about pardoning the Chalcidians?

Was it appropriate for Titus to sometimes exercise the "heat of his words?" How did he keep his inclination to speak out from going too far? (Ephesians 4:26: Be ye angry, and sin not: let not the sun go down upon your wrath.)

Lesson Eleven

Introduction

The story continues with themes of personal bitterness and revenge.

Who annoyed whom first?

The structure of this passage is a bit confusing. Titus was elected censor in 189 BC. Marcus Cato the Elder was censor in 184 BC. So Titus (as censor) first annoyed Cato by passing him over for leader of the Senate; and then five years later, Cato "cleaned house" in the Senate and expelled Titus's brother Lucius.

Vocabulary

    censor: see notes for Marcus Cato the Censor

    tribune of the people: a representative of the commoners in the Roman Senate

    Marcus Porcius Cato: see Plutarch's *Life of Marcus Cato the Censor*

    prince of the Senate: first member of the Senate

    redound: reflect (badly) on him

    the marketplace: the Roman Forum

    the pulpit for orations: the place for public speaking

    by practise he procured of the Senate: he arranged it

    were called in, and made void: cancelled

Reading

Furthermore, after Titus had done these things, and that the war with Antiochus was ended, he was chosen **censor** at Rome, with the son of that same Marcellus, who had been five times consul. This office is of great dignity, and as a man may say, the crown of all the honours that a citizen of Rome can have in their commonwealth. They put of the Senate, four men only: but they were not famous. They did receive all into the number of citizens of Rome, that would present themselves to be enrolled in their common register: with a proviso, that they were born free by father and mother. They were compelled to do it, by Terentius Culeo, **tribune of the people**, who to despite the nobility, persuaded the people of Rome to command it so.

Now at that time, two of the noblest and most famous men of Rome were great enemies one against another: Publius Scipio African[us], and **Marcus Porcius Cato**. Of these two, Titus named Publius Scipio African[us], to be **prince of the Senate**, as the chiefest and worthiest person in the city: and got the displeasure of the other, which was Cato, by this mishap. Titus had a brother [*a member of the Senate*] called Lucius Quintius Flamininus, nothing like unto him in condition at all: for he was so dissolutely and licentiously given over to his pleasure, that he forgot all comeliness and honesty. [*His extreme misbehaviour is omitted here.*]

Howsoever it was, Marcus Cato [*when he was later*] chosen censor, and cleansing the Senate of all unworthy persons, he [also expelled] Lucius Quintius Flamininus, although he had been consul: which disgrace did seem to **redound** to his brother Titus Quintius Flamininus also. Whereupon both the brethren came weeping with all humility before the people, and made a petition that seemed very reasonable and civil: which was that they would command Cato to come before them, to declare the cause openly why he had with such open shame defaced so noble a house as theirs was. Cato then without delay, or shrinking back, came with his companion [*the other consul*] into **the marketplace**, where he asked Titus out aloud, if he knew nothing of the [unspeakable event]. Titus answered, he knew not of it. Then Cato opened all the whole matter as it was, and in the end of his tale, he bade Lucius Quintius swear openly, if he would deny that [what] he had said was true. Lucius answered not a word. Whereupon the people judged the shame was justly laid upon him: and so to honour Cato, they did accompany him from **the pulpit for orations**, home unto his own house. But Titus being much offended at the disgrace of his brother, became enemy to Cato [*i.e. more than he was before*], and fell in with those that of long time had hated him. And so **by practise he procured of the Senate**, that all bargains of leases, and all deeds of sales made by Cato during his [*previous*] office,

were called in, and made void: and caused many suits also to be commenced against him. Wherein, I cannot say he did wisely or civilly, to become mortal enemy to an honest man, a good citizen, and dutiful in his office, for his year, [for an] unworthy kinsman, who had justly deserved the shame laid upon him.

Notwithstanding, shortly after when the people were assembled in the theater to see games played, and the Senators were set according to their custom, in the most honourable places: Lucius Flamininus came in also, who in lowly and humble manner went to sit down in the furthest seats of the theater, without regard of his former honour: which when the people saw, they took pity of him, and could not abide to see him thus dishonoured. So they cried out to have him come and sit among the other Senators and consuls, who made him place, and received him accordingly.

Narration and Discussion

"Wherein, I cannot say he did wisely or civilly, to become mortal enemy to an honest man, a good citizen, and dutiful in his office, for his year, [for an] unworthy kinsman, who had justly deserved the shame laid upon him." How far should we go to defend a relative or a close friend, if he or she deserves punishment? (Two Bible passages to think about: David's reaction to the death of his traitorous son Absalom; and Abraham's intercession for his nephew Lot.)

Lesson Twelve

Introduction

People thought Titus a little crazy to take on the "youthful violence" of battle at his advanced age. But it seemed that former glories were not enough to satisfy him, especially when there was the chance of capturing an old enemy.

Vocabulary

far unmeet: quite unsuitable

Titus Flamininus

Hannibal: (247-183/182/181 B.C., it's unsure) was a famous Punic Carthaginian military commander, and an old enemy of Titus Flamininus.

faint heart: fickleness towards him

privy caves and vaults: secret tunnels!

all the vents out, had watch and ward upon them: all the ways out (that no-one was supposed to know about) were being guarded

Pyrrhus: King of Epirus from 307-302 and 295-272 B.C.

clemency: forgiveness

he parled with him of peace: he had peace talks with him

So divers greatly commending the goodly sayings and deeds of Scipio: So with many people greatly commending, etc.

in discharge of Titus: in clearing him of blame

Aristonicus: the pretender to the throne of Pergamon; the name he took as king was Eumenes III. The former king had bequeathed (left) his kingdom to the Romans, but the Romans were slow to secure their claim, and Aristonicus stepped in.

Mithridates: Mithridates V of Pontus

ambassade: mission

Reading

But to return again to Titus. The natural ambition and covetous greedy mind he had of honour, was very well taken and esteemed, so long as he had any occasion offered him to exercise it in the wars, which we have spoken of before. For, after he had been consul, of his own seeking he became a colonel of a thousand footmen, not being called to it by any man. So when he began to stoop for age, and that he had given over as a man at the last cast, to bear office any longer in the state: they saw plainly he was ambitious beyond measure, to suffer himself in old age to be overcome with such youthful violence, being **far unmeet** for any of his years. For methinks his ambition was the only cause that moved him to procure

Hannibal's death, which bred him much disliking and ill opinion with many.

For, after Hannibal had fled out of his own country, he went first unto king Antiochus: who, after he lost the battle in Phrygia, was glad the Romans granted him peace with such conditions as themselves would. Wherefore Hannibal fled again from him, and after he had long wandered up and down, at the length he came to the realm of Bithynia, and remained there about King Prusias, the Romans knowing it well enough: and because Hannibal was then an old broken man, of no force nor power, and one whom fortune had spurned at her feet, they made no more reckoning of him. But Titus being sent Ambassador by the Senate, unto Prusias king of Bithynia, and finding Hannibal there, it grieved him to see him alive. So that notwithstanding Prusias marvellously entreated him, to take pity upon Hannibal, a poor old man, and his friend who came to him for succour: yet he could not persuade Titus to be content he should live. Hannibal long before had received answer of his death from an oracle, to this effect:

> The land of Libya, shall cover under mould,
> The valiant corpse of Hannibal, when he is dead and cold.

So Hannibal understood that of Libya, as if he should have died in Africa, and been buried in Carthage.

There is a certain sandy country in Bithynia near to the seaside, where there is a little village called Libyssa, and where Hannibal remained continually. He, mistrusting King Prusias' **faint heart**, and fearing the Romans' malice also, had made seven **privy caves and vaults** under ground long before, that he might secretly go out at either of them which way he would, and every one of them came to the main vault where himself did lie, and could not be discerned outwardly. When it was told him that Titus had willed Prusias to deliver him into his hands, he sought then to save himself by those means: but he found that **all the vents out, had watch and ward upon them** by the king's commandment. So then he determined to kill himself.

Now some say, that he wound a linen towel hard about his neck, and commanded one of his men he should set his knee upon his buttock, and weighing hard upon him, holding the towel fast he should pull his neck backward with all the power and strength he could, and never [stop] pressing on him, till he had strangled him.

Titus Flamininus

Other say that he drank bull's blood, as Midas and Themistocles had done before him. But Titus Livius writeth, that he had poison which he kept for such a purpose, and tempered it in a cup he held in his hands, and before he drank, he spake these words: Come on, let us deliver the Romans of this great care, since my life is so grievous to them, that they think it too long to tarry the natural death of a poor old man, whom they hate so much: and yet Titus by this shall win no honourable victory, nor worthy the memory of the ancient Romans, who advertised **King Pyrrhus** their enemy, even when he made wars with them, and had won battles of them, that he should beware of poisoning which was intended towards him. And this was Hannibal's end, as we find it written.

The news whereof being come to Rome unto the Senate, many of them thought Titus too violent and cruel, to have made Hannibal kill himself in that sort, when extremity of age had overcome him already, and was as a bird left naked, her feathers falling from her for age: and so much the more, because there was no instant occasion offered him to urge him to do it, but a covetous mind of honour, for that he would be chronicled to be the cause and author of Hannibal's death.

And then in contrariwise they did much honour and commend the **clemency** and noble mind of Scipio Africanus. Who having overcome Hannibal in battle, in Africa [him]self, and being then indeed to be feared, and had been never overcome before: yet he did not cause him to be driven out of his country, neither did ask him of the Carthaginians, but both then, and before the battle, when he **parled with him of peace**, he took Hannibal courteously by the hand, and after the battle, in the conditions of peace he gave them, he never spake word of hurt to Hannibal's person, neither did he shew any cruelty to him in his misery. And they tell how afterwards they met again together in the city of Ephesus, and as they were walking, that Hannibal took the upper hand of Scipio: and that Scipio bare it patiently, and left not of walking for that, neither shewed any countenance of misliking. And in entering into discourse of many matters, they descended in the end to talk of ancient captains: and Hannibal gave judgement, that Alexander the Great was the famousest captain, **Pyrrhus** the second, and himself the third. Then Scipio smiling, gently asked him: What wouldst thou say then, if I had not overcome thee? Truly, quoth Hannibal, I would not then put myself the third man, but the first, and above all the captains that ever were.

So divers greatly commending the goodly sayings and deeds of Scipio, did marvellously mislike Titus, for that he had (as a man may say) laid his hands upon the death of another man. Other[s] to the contrary again said, it was well done of him, saying, that Hannibal so long as he lived, was a fire to the Empire of the Romans, which lacked but one to blow it [*into a dangerous fire*]: and that when he was in his best force and lusty age, it was not his hand nor body that troubled the Romans, so much, but his great wisdom and skill he had in the wars, and the mortal hate he bare in his heart towards the Romans, which neither years, neither age would diminish or take away. For men's natural conditions do remain still, but fortune doth not always keep in a state, but changeth still, and then quickeneth up our desires to set willingly upon those that war against us, because they hate us in their hearts.

The things which fell out afterwards, did greatly prove the reasons brought out for this purpose, **in discharge of Titus**.

For one **Aristonicus**, son of a daughter of a player upon the zither, under the fame and glory of Eumenes, whose [illegitimate son] he was, filled all Asia with war and rebellion, by reason the people rose in his favour. Again **Mithridates**, after so many losses he had received against Sylla and Fimbria, and after so many armies overthrown by battle and wars, and after so many famous captains lost and killed: did yet recover again, and came to be of great power both by sea and land against Lucullus.

Truly Hannibal was no lower brought than Caius Marius had been. For he had a king to his friend, that gave him entertainment for him and his family, and made him Admiral of his ships, and general of his horsemen and footmen in the field. Marius also went up and down Africa a-begging for his living, insomuch as his enemies at Rome mocked him to scorn: and soon after notwithstanding they fell down at his feet before him, when they saw they were whipped, murdered, and slain within Rome by his commandment.

Thus we see no man can say certainly he is mean or great, by reason of the uncertainty of things to come: considering there is but one death, and change of better life. Some say also, that Titus did not [do] this act alone, and of his own authority: but that he was sent Ambassador with Lucius Scipio to no other end, but to put Hannibal to death, by what means soever they could. Furthermore after this **ambassade**, we do not find any notable thing written of Titus worthy of memory, neither in peace, nor in wars. For he died quietly of natural death at home in his country.

Narration and Discussion

To what extent was Titus responsible for the death of Hannibal? Should old men still be considered potentially dangerous?

Do you find the end, focusing more on Hannibal than on Titus, somewhat disappointing or anticlimactic? Even Lesson Eleven ended with people cheering for Titus's brother rather than himself. Your assignment: go back through the Life, and choose two or three quotes that describe the best of Titus Quintius Flamininus. Be prepared to explain why you chose the ones you did.

The Plutarch Project

Bibliography

Mason, Charlotte M. 1886. *Home Education*. Reprint, with foreword by John Thorley. Wheaton, IL: Tyndale House, 1989.

Mason, Charlotte M. 1896. *Parents and Children*. Reprint, with foreword by John Thorley. Wheaton, IL: Tyndale House, 1989.

Plutarch's Lives of the Noble Greeks and Romans. Englished by Sir Thomas North. With an introduction by George Wyndham. Third Volume. London: Dent, 1895.
https://archive.org/details/livesenglishedb03plut

Plutarch's Lives: The Dryden Plutarch. Revised by Arthur Hugh Clough. Volume 2. London: J.M. Dent, 1910.
https://archive.org/details/plutarchslives02plut

About the Author

Anne E. White (www.annewrites.ca) has shared her knowledge of Charlotte Mason's methods through magazine columns, online writing, and conference workshops. She is an Advisory member of AmblesideOnline, and the author of *Minds More Awake: The Vision of Charlotte Mason*.